PRESENTED TO

_____

BY

_____

DATE

_____

OCEAN SYMPHONY, TERRIGAL, NEW SOUTH WALES, AUSTRALIA

Tough times never last, but tough people do!

ROBERT H. SCHULLER

Power for Life
DAILY DEVOTIONAL

HOUR OF POWER

Energize Your Positive Faith Day by Day

Featuring contributions from

ROBERT ANTHONY SCHULLER

and

ROBERT HAROLD SCHULLER

and

SHEILA SCHULLER COLEMAN

and excerpts from

POWER FOR LIFE BIBLE

with

PANOGRAPHS BY KEN DUNCAN

DR. ROBERT ANTHONY SCHULLER

Introduction

As I meet people or receive e-mails and letters from people around the world who have been touched by our ministry at the Crystal Cathedral and the televised *Hour of Power*, I am constantly amazed at how many of them credit the positive lives they lead to spending time with God on a daily basis.

In this special *Hour of Power* devotional, you will find an entire year's worth of daily reflections that were written to energize your faith, restore your hope, and reassure you of the enduring love of God. Each devotional includes a stunning Panograph taken by our great friend Ken Duncan, a key verse from Scripture, and a short devotional message that is meant to help you tap in to the power and love of God.

Covering a variety of topics, these short devotionals will bring a smile to your face, offer you a timely word of encouragement, inspire a thought, or provide you with a fresh insight from God's word that relates to everyday life. They have been gleaned from some of the Schuller family's books and messages as well as from excerpts of the *Power for Life Bible* from the Crystal Cathedral.

My hope is that you will take a few minutes each day to refresh your faith and find new power for life by connecting with God using this book as your daily guide.

Let God's power come alive in you this year!

ROBERT ANTHONY SCHULLER, SENIOR PASTOR
CRYSTAL CATHEDRAL, HOUR OF POWER   www.hourofpower.org

WHITSUNDAY ISLANDS, QUEENSLAND, AUSTRALIA

You are an immortal being, created for eternity.
Therefore, the journey is your never-ending destination.

ROBERT A. SCHULLER

Foreword

Wʰat an honor and a pleasure it has been to provide the images to accompany the profound inspirational text of this book. While selecting the images I was continually overwhelmed with the insight that has come from the Schullers' many years of life experience in ministry.

I believe this devotional book will be a real power source of blessing to all who journey through its pages. The Schullers have really shared from their hearts in this publication and their encouragement will truly inspire people.

What I love about the Schullers and the Crystal Cathedral ministries is that when any of them say, "God loves you and so do I," they really mean it. That is what has endeared their ministry to me—and I know millions of others—as they shine the love of Jesus.

Nothing is impossible with Jesus. | KEN DUNCAN

Contents

POWER FOR LIFE DAILY DEVOTIONAL *Energize Your Positive Faith Day by Day* First published 2008 for *Hour of Power* by Panographs Publishing Pty Ltd ABN 21 050 235 606 PO Box 3015 Wamberal NSW 2260 Australia Telephone +61 2 4367 6777 ©2008. Panographs Publishing Pty Ltd. All rights reserved. No portion of this book may be reproduced, stored in a retrieval system, or transmitted in any form or by any means—electronic, mechanical, photocopying, recording, or any other—without the prior written permission of Panographs Publishing Pty Ltd. Panographs is a registered trademark of the Ken Duncan Group Pty Limited. Most scripture quotations used in this book are from *Today's New International Version®* Copyright ©2001, 2005 by International Bible Society. Used by permission. All rights reserved. Photography by Ken Duncan ©2008 Divine Guidance P/L Designed by Good Catch Design Reprographics by CFL Print Studio Printed and bound by Everbest Printing Co Ltd., China ISBN 9780980445381 To view the range of Ken Duncan's panoramic Limited Edition Prints visit the Ken Duncan Gallery online: www.kenduncan.com To visit the *Hour of Power* website: www.hourofpower.org

FULL MOON, EAST CORINTH, VERMONT, USA

It doesn't matter who or what is against you,
because God is with you and always on your side!

ROBERT A. SCHULLER

January

THE TWELVE APOSTLES, VICTORIA, AUSTRALIA

New beginnings

*"Put on the new self,
created to be like God in true righteousness and holiness."*

EPHESIANS 4:24

A blank slate. A new semester. A fresh start.

What do all these share in common? A chance to start over! What a powerful opportunity it is when you are able to put aside the old false starts...the dead ends...the disappointments. The old has passed the new day is here! You don't have to be shackled by the past when you have a beautiful future before you. That is the powerful message of Christianity. And the New Year reminds you that your past has been redeemed, and as a result you can face tomorrow with joyful anticipation!

So...grab hold of this powerful opportunity! Don't let it slip it away! Take advantage of Christ's offer for a new beginning. Start today to build a powerful new tomorrow—with God's help! | SHEILA SCHULLER COLEMAN

WONDER LAKE, DENALI NATIONAL PARK, ALASKA, USA

Just a thought

"By the word of the Lord the heavens were made,
their starry host by the breath of his mouth."

PSALM 33:6

Our magnificent world began with just a thought. All God had to do was think it—and it happened. He didn't have to strategically plan with a committee, draw architectural blueprints, or put in endless hours. No, all he had to do was think it.

God was pleased with what he made. An artist rarely likes what he or she has painted. Even the masters, such as Rembrandt and Monet, were frustrated with their works of art. But after creating the world, God looked at what he made and "saw that it was good."

Imagine the power it took for God to think about the galaxies, the glorious oceans, waves, volcanoes, and beautiful earth in all of its majesty. Yet all of this was created with just a thought.

Our God is an awesome, omnipotent, all-powerful God.

| POWER FOR LIFE BIBLE

KIMBERLEY FALLS, WESTERN AUSTRALIA, AUSTRALIA

Look and see

*"Since the creation of the world God's invisible qualities…
have been clearly seen, being understood from what has been made,
so that people are without excuse."*

ROMANS 1:20

Some people think God isn't concerned with the minute details of life. They believe God set the universe in motion, as if he were winding some giant watch spring, and then went off and left man to fend for himself. This couldn't be farther from the truth.

Just take a look around. If you do, you'll see God's loving care built into nature in a myriad of amazing ways.

Take earth, for instance. It is delicately balanced in space like a fragile house of cards that was built with the utmost care. The fact that it sustains human life is an incredible miracle.

If looking outward isn't enough to convince you of God's loving care, then take a look inside at the intricate workings of the human body.

All creation shouts, "God loves you and he built this world to bless you!"

| ROBERT A. SCHULLER

PALM ISLAND, QUEENSLAND, AUSTRALIA

God's fingerprints

*"In the beginning
you laid the foundations of the earth,
and the heavens are the work of your hands."*

PSALM 102:25

When astronaut John Glenn returned to space, one thing that struck him was how thin and fragile our atmosphere is. If our planet were smaller it couldn't support an atmosphere like that on Mercury. If it were larger, the atmosphere would contain free hydrogen, which is poison for us. Earth is the only planet with an atmosphere that can support human, animal and plant life. An accident? Not a chance!

The unmistakable fingerprints of a divine Creator are all over the universe. We are surrounded by fantastic displays of God's creativity and craftsmanship. To say that the universe happened by chance is absurd. Its design, intricacy and orderliness point to a personally involved Creator—one who cares about you and what happens to you. The Creator cries out from his creation—"I did all this for you." | ROBERT H. SCHULLER

CUDMIRRAH BEACH, NEW SOUTH WALES, AUSTRALIA

God's better idea

*"Lord, our Lord,
how majestic is your name in all the earth!
You have set your glory above the heavens."*

PSALM 8:1

If God could create our majestic world with just a thought, what about the problems you are facing today? Whether financial struggles, marital issues, health concerns, or even life-threatening cancer, our omnipotent God is just a prayer away. The God who created our universe is your helper, so reach out to him and claim his help.

Claim big things. Claim healing. Claim joy. Claim peace. He will not turn a deaf ear to your pleas for help. He wants the best for us, his children. He loves to delight and surprise us. Even if things turn out *different* than we would have thought, God's thoughts are *better*. It's not unusual for him to have a better idea.

So look at the heavens, look at this majestic world, and remember that God will help you. | POWER FOR LIFE BIBLE

MYALL LAKES, NEW SOUTH WALES, AUSTRALIA

In the beginning

"Jesus said, 'I am the light of the world.
Whoever follows me will never walk in darkness,
but will have the light of life.'"

JOHN 8:12

Have you ever been in a room with no windows or doors and turned off the lights? It's pitch dark. But if you were to take a light into that dark room—no matter where in the room you put the light, and no matter how small the light—the darkness could not hide the light.

Genesis 1 teaches us about the importance and value of light. In the beginning, God separated the light from the darkness. Before that, the earth was formless and empty...and darkness covered its surface.

We tend to be afraid of the dark. Good news! God always overcomes the darkness because he is the Light. When the light of God shines in the dark places of our lives, the power of the Light transforms our lives from nothing to something.

In the beginning, God created...LIGHT! And with light, came hope.

| ROBERT A. SCHULLER

JULIA PFEIFFER BURNS STATE PARK, CALIFORNIA, USA

A time for every season

"Holy, holy, holy is the Lord Almighty;
the whole earth is full of his glory."

ISAIAH 6:3

In California, we love our mountains, seashores, palm trees, and orange groves. But we also love our deserts. In the summertime, visitors drive through the deserts and see them as bleak, barren, hot, lifeless places. But native Californians know that hidden beneath the swirling sands and dry gravel is an abundance of fertile seed.

With spring comes a riot of color throughout the desert. Acres of brilliant, blooming flowers cover the once lifeless domain with rolling seas of flaming color.

Then comes fall and winter when blossoms wither, leaving seeds to be awakened once again when raindrops fall, holding the promise of a delightful future.

What is history but the story of humankind discovering and rediscovering riches that were here all along? Still more amazing is the reality that the greatest gifts, left untouched inside God's great earth, have yet to be discovered. | ROBERT H. SCHULLER

PIPELINE, OAHU, HAWAII, USA

Created with divine splendor

"You made them a little lower than the angels;
you crowned them with glory and honor."

HEBREWS 2:7

Making a transatlantic flight to Madrid, Spain, I was seated next to a medical doctor from Poland who was of the Jewish faith. I asked, "Do you believe in God?"

"Indeed I do," she replied.

Later I inquired, "What's the difference between man, animals, and the other higher primates?"

Her response came quickly: "While at medical school in Warsaw, my professor told us, 'The difference between man and all other primates and animals is that man has the capacity to believe in God. He wanted all of his creatures to know they were created by him, so he picked his highest form of creature—the human being—and gave him the capacity to understand that God is behind it all.'"

We alone are capable of believing in God. It is through us that God fulfills his plans and purposes in this world. | ROBERT H. SCHULLER

ST MARY LAKE, GLACIER NATIONAL PARK, MONTANA, USA

Authority for life

"Scripture says…'God himself has put everything under Christ.'"

1 CORINTHIANS 15:27

During the early '80s a series of E.F. Hutton commercials aired on television. In one ad, two people are sitting in a crowded, noisy restaurant when one says to the other, "My broker is E.F. Hutton." The restaurant falls silent as everyone leans forward to hear what the man will say next. The commercial ends with, "When E.F. Hutton speaks, people listen."

In the account of Creation found in Genesis 1:1–2:4, we read these words nine times: "God said…and it was so." When God spoke in Creation he was taking supreme authority and ownership over everything he spoke into existence. He made the things we can see and the things we cannot see. "Everything was created through him and for him" (Colossians 1:16).

Christ has supreme ownership and authority over your life. Will you trust him with your life—all of it? | ROBERT A. SCHULLER

DENALI NATIONAL PARK, ALASKA, USA

Wonderfully made

"I praise you because I am fearfully and wonderfully made."

PSALM 139:14

The pinnacle of God's creation, even more majestic than earth itself, is the creation that means the most to him—you! God was pleased with his creation. After he created the heavens, he said, *"This is good!"* After he created the earth and the animals, he said, *"This is good!"* And when he created you and me, he said, *"This is good!"* We are God's children, his masterpiece, and we have all been fearfully and wonderfully made.

Too often, however, we fail to appreciate the unique and valued individuals that we are. We compare ourselves and try to measure up to others or try to be the kind of person we think we need to be. Look in the mirror today and say in unison with God, your Creator, *"This is good!"*

| POWER FOR LIFE BIBLE

WAILUA FALLS, KAUAI, HAWAII, USA

Soul food

*"When I consider your heavens, the work of your fingers,
the moon and the stars, which you have set in place, what are mere mortals
that you are mindful of them, human beings that you care for them?"*

PSALM 8:3-4

Beauty is not a luxury. *Beauty is essential*; it is food to our souls. Without beauty we become spiritually malnourished. As with food, we can get by on empty calories for a while, but eventually it will catch up to us and we will find ourselves becoming weak and unable to stay focused or be as healthy and productive as we want to be. So it is with beauty. We can work or live in a harsh, cluttered environment for only so long before our souls become weary and our passion wanes.

Nourish your soul daily. Take a walk through the park, spend time in the garden, sit on the beach, read the beautiful language of God's word, or watch the majesty of a sunrise or sunset. When you do, you will plug into the power of the God who created this majestic world. | POWER FOR LIFE BIBLE

SCUDDER SCHOOL, PRAIRIE SONG, OKLAHOMA, USA

Lord, teach me!

"Teach me your way, O Lord, and I will walk in your truth."

PSALM 86:11

When my daughter Christina was five years old and learning how to spell and write, she loved to ask me, "Daddy, how do you spell red?" I'd begin, "R." She'd repeat "R" and write the letter. I'd continue, "E." And she'd write "E." And I'd end, "D." And she'd complete the word. Meanwhile my son Anthony, who was then four, listened to our exchange. One day he asked, "Daddy, how do you spell black?" I began, "B." To which he responded, "Daddy, what's a 'B'?"

We all need help learning to spell—to operate in the ways of God's kingdom. We ask, "Lord, how do you spell *loving*?" He responds, "L." At first we may need to ask, "What's an 'L'?" because we're clueless about his ways. But the good news is, as we spend time with him, God teaches us his ways.

| ROBERT A. SCHULLER

LOG CABIN, PELLA, IOWA, USA

A new recipe for life

"Blessed are those who trust in the Lord,
whose confidence is in him."

JEREMIAH 17:7

One fond childhood memory I have is that of my mother baking apple pies, kneading bread dough, and mixing up one of her fabulous desserts. Mom never used a recipe; it was all in her head. She would catch a little flour in her hand and sprinkle it in, give the saltshaker a few shakes, or pour a splash of vanilla extract into the mixture. I always felt a little uneasy as I watched her work.

She would smile confidently and tell me, "Don't worry, Bob—it will come out right!"

Faith is like that. We mix the ingredients before we're sure what the outcome will be. Faith declares boldly, "I am trusting God *and* myself" to mix all of life's ingredients together in a way that will produce something glorious.

Go ahead—dare to dream up a new recipe for life!

| ROBERT H. SCHULLER

SEQUOIA, SEQUOIA NATIONAL PARK, CALIFORNIA, USA

A new creation

"If anyone is in Christ, the new creation has come:
The old has gone, the new is here!"

2 CORINTHIANS 5:17

Who doesn't like to replace the old with the new? Who doesn't like a new pair of shoes, a new car, or a new book? Who can hold a new baby without smiling? Even though you know that the new will eventually become old, that newness is fleeting, you can enjoy it, knowing it won't be the last time.

Life's cycles repeatedly include newness. There's always hope of something new. After each night there's a new day. The end of each story offers the beginning of a new one. At the end of each journey is the start of a new adventure.

God specializes in making you someone new. Through his grace he gives you the power to put off the old life and become a new creation. Accept the gift of a new life through Christ today! | SHEILA SCHULLER COLEMAN

SAND DUNES, WESTERN AUSTRALIA, AUSTRALIA

Footprints in the sand

"When you pass through the waters,
I will be with you; and when you pass through the rivers,
they will not sweep over you."

ISAIAH 43:2

It took a lot of faith for Moses to lead the Israelites out of Egypt. And it took an equal amount of faith for the Israelites to follow God. But as they stepped out in faith and put their footprints on the floor of the Red Sea, they left a lesson for us to follow: Walk in faith, believing that the God of miracles will not let you down.

Commit your way to God. He will keep you from harm. Even when you stumble, he will catch you and keep you from falling. He will take every apparent mistake and redeem it. And if you've been deeply wounded, God will heal you and use your wound for his good purposes.

So, step out in faith. Run like a child joyfully through life, holding on to the protective strong hand of God Almighty. | POWER FOR LIFE BIBLE

LIFEGUARD TOWER, SIESTA BEACH, FLORIDA, USA

Birth of faith

"Faith…is not from yourselves, it is the gift of God."

EPHESIANS 2:8

Disappointment's seeds of doubt can burrow, thrive, and threaten to choke out your faith. Where was God when you needed him? Why hasn't the dream he gave you succeeded? Did you hear him wrong? Did you lack the skills? Did he abandon you?

Faith isn't faith until it's tested. Faith bridges the gap between the circumstances that are true today and God's eternal truth. Faith carries you through tough times believing they will pass and that you will emerge to see the beauty that was part of God's plan all along.

How do you keep believing when you see no results, or worse, when no miracle happens, and God takes a loved one home too early for your liking? Then, you make a choice—to believe anyway. Nurture faith today by saying, "I believe! I believe! I believe!" | SHEILA SCHULLER COLEMAN

FRUIT MARKETS, TURKEY

Garden-fresh faith

"Keep hold of the deep truths of the faith."

1 TIMOTHY 3:9

Yummm. Fresh tomatoes...fresh lettuce...fresh sweet corn...is there anything more enticing than garden-fresh vegetables or flowers? How about oven-fresh bread with butter melting into the warm crevices? Conversely, is there anything less appetizing than stale, moldy dry goods, or flowers souring in a bacteria-laden vase?

Keeping faith garden-fresh is as easy as breathing in the Spirit of God, the spirit of faith, and exhaling the spirit of doubt. It's as easy as reading a verse or two of God's love letter, as easy as a moment of prayer in God's house or your backyard garden.

Keeping faith garden-fresh is as easy as keeping your faith watered by God's Spirit, fed by God's word, warmed by the sunshine of God's love, so that your garden-fresh faith can bring inspiring encouragement to your family, your neighbors, and your coworkers—not to mention, yourself!

| SHEILA SCHULLER COLEMAN

GARRAPATA STATE PARK, CALIFORNIA, USA

More than conquerors

"In all these things we are more than conquerors through him who loved us."

ROMANS 8:37

Charlie Plumb was a prisoner of war for 2,103 days! Two things kept him sane: Communicating with God and communicating with a cell mate, Bob Shoemaker, who dug a small hole in his cell wall and wove a wire through it.

Bob and Charlie began their communication by inventing a code and tugging on the wire. The first thing Bob said to Charlie was: "It sounds like you're suffering from prison thinking. You're feeling sorry for yourself and are blaming other people. That kind of thinking is fatal. Faith is the only way to beat it. You have to tap into a source of power that is greater than yourself." And he added, "If you've got *faith*, you'll make it."

When faced with desperate situations cling to this truth: "In all things we are more than conquerors through him who loved us."

| ROBERT H. SCHULLER

HORSESHOE BEND, COLORADO RIVER, ARIZONA, USA

Serendipities

"See, I am doing a new thing…
I am making a way in the desert and streams in the wasteland."

ISAIAH 43:19

Serendipities are those unexpected, surprising experiences God ushers into our life. Sometimes they change our life completely. Other times, they may only add another piece to a puzzle we've worked on for years.

History is filled with examples of serendipities. Take Dr. Harry Coover for instance. In 1941, he came up with a compound in the Kodak laboratory when trying to create a clear plastic. Unfortunately, the cyanoacrylate he was using was too sticky, so he shelved it. Then in 1951, he and an associate took a second look at it, and accidentally stuck a very expensive pair of lenses together. Eventually that mishap led to a new product which Harry Coover introduced into the market in 1958–Super Glue.

Every day is a new adventure guided by a good God who loves to surprise his children with unexpected "serendipities" along the way. | ROBERT A. SCHULLER

JENNE FARM, VERMONT, USA

Beginning is half done

"She thought, 'If I just touch his clothes...'"

MARK 5:28

This concept has been the saving grace of many graduate students or leaders of ambitious projects. Tilling the soil portends planting a garden and reaping the harvest. Applying online for an academic program is the first step toward earning that degree you've always wanted. Putting pen to paper is the first step toward writing the book that's on your heart.

Sure, the road that stretches from that point will be long and bumpy. Of course, it may take years to finish and reach your goal. But there is a psychological principle at work in taking the first step. By beginning you have a start toward making your dream a reality. You have overcome the hardest hurdle—avoiding taking the first step for fear of failure. Now that you are on your way, there will be no stopping you!

| SHEILA SCHULLER COLEMAN

ULURU, NORTHERN TERRITORY, AUSTRALIA

Blessings that endure

"Such is the destiny of all who forget God;
so perishes the hope of the godless."

JOB 8:13

At twenty-seven years of age, he was hailed as a genius by music critics worldwide. He was worth millions of dollars and besieged by adoring fans everywhere he went. He was the father of a beautiful baby girl.

Kurt Cobain had everything in the world going for him. But it wasn't enough. One April evening in his luxurious home in Seattle, the leader of the rock group Nirvana killed himself with a gun. By the world's standards, Kurt Cobain was a tremendous success. Sadly, for him it wasn't enough. Yes, he was successful, but he never felt blessed.

Ironic, isn't it, how those people we often most admire or wish we could trade places with are really miserable deep inside.

The blessings the world gives may last for a season, but the blessings of God will endure forever. | ROBERT A. SCHULLER

FISHERMEN AT TWILIGHT, SEA OF GALILEE, ISRAEL

The call

"Then Jesus said…, 'Don't be afraid; from now on you will fish for people.'
So they pulled their boats up on shore, left everything and followed him."

LUKE 5:10-11

Jesus chose twelve men to accompany him during his ministry. These were men that he mentored, encouraged, and equipped to carry on the ministry after he returned to heaven. He chose eleven fishermen and one tax collector.

Jesus still calls people to follow him. The call is much more than a career, or an occupation—it is a call to live for him wherever we are. In following him as his modern-day disciples, we can ask ourselves in all situations, "What would Jesus want me to do?"

One thing we can do is to become a fisher of men (and women) by inviting them to church. Ninety percent of people report that they would go to church if someone would invite them. Cast out your net, dust off your fishing pole, and start fishing. You'll be amazed at who you might catch!

| POWER FOR LIFE BIBLE

OMEO VALLEY, VICTORIA, AUSTRALIA

Destiny or destination?

"We declare God's wisdom,
a mystery that...God destined for our glory before time began."

1 C O R I N T H I A N S   2 : 7

Colonel Sanders, founder of Kentucky Fried Chicken, was sixty-five years old when he lost everything he owned. He had a tiny chicken shack on the side of the road. Then a major highway came through the area and completely bypassed his little restaurant. All he had left was a recipe for fried chicken.

He didn't plan to found a billion-dollar restaurant chain, but when Colonel Sanders was stripped of what little he had accumulated over the years, he considered his options, decided he had something of value, and used that to take his next step.

You don't decide your destiny. Things happen. Outcomes occur. All you decide is your next step. Then God uses that to craft the destiny he has in mind for you. When you live in the Spirit, God directs your steps in ways you cannot imagine! | ROBERT A. SCHULLER

MOUNT RUSHMORE, SOUTH DAKOTA, USA

The power of the human spirit

"With your help I can advance against a troop;
with my God I can scale a wall."

PSALM 18:29

The power of the human spirit is inexplicable. Jesus Christ has been my source of inspiration. Through his life, Jesus demonstrated how the human spirit can face and overcome human suffering. Jesus died on a cross in pain and shame, yet did not for even a moment give in to hatred. "Father, forgive them" was his response. He looked ahead with hope.

With faith in God, we can do the same. We can come from nowhere and go anywhere. We can shine like a bright light as we move through dark times and face the worst life throws at us. Everyone who holds onto faith during times of disaster will endure and will be embraced with affection and respect by the people around them.

You are a force to be reckoned with when your faith is intact and God is empowering you. | ROBERT H. SCHULLER

MONUMENT VALLEY, ARIZONA, USA

Building your faith muscle

"Stand firm in the faith;
be men of courage; be strong."

1 CORINTHIANS 16:13

I t's easy to dream big if all you have to do is sit on the bench. But you can't make a basket from the bench. You can't win the game from the locker room. You have to suit up and get onto the court of life. And that takes courage! Not to mention hard work.

If a basketball player is working out to get in top physical shape with the dream of winning the tournament, then hasn't the dream built the player? In the same way, when you exercise your faith, taking risky steps in the process, your faith will grow. When you dare to follow God into new arenas, you put muscle on your faith. Your dreams force your faith to become stronger, more powerful. If more faith is the only result of a God-given dream, isn't this alone worth it? | SHEILA SCHULLER COLEMAN

SAND DUNES, SOSSUSVLEI, NAMIBIA

Dream big

*"Joseph had a dream…'Listen,' he said…
'the sun and moon and eleven stars were bowing down to me.'"*

GENESIS 37:5-9

Dare to grab a dream—a big dream—a bold dream! You may get dragged along by it because dreams often provide impetus, forcing growth. Dreams build your faith, but they also build your skills and abilities.

If you dream of being a teacher, you will have to return to school and earn a teaching certificate. If you dream of revitalizing a struggling organization, you must learn new aspects of organizational leadership. It is impossible to build a big, audacious dream without the dream pushing you to grow and learn.

The more experienced and equipped you are, the more you can do for God. Don't wait to be fully equipped before you dare to dream. Start now. Dream big. Then grab hold of the dream and the dream will propel you to become the equipped power tool God needs you to be. | SHEILA SCHULLER COLEMAN

SKYSCAPE, SOUTH AUSTRALIA, AUSTRALIA

Be encouraged

"Encourage one another, be of one mind, live in peace.
And the God of love and peace will be with you."

2   C O R I N T H I A N S   1 3 : 1 1

It's the rare person who hasn't failed in what he or she wanted to do at some point. We all make mistakes. And some of those mistakes have serious consequences for us and for others. But if we learn from our mistakes and turn our lives around, we can turn a negative into a positive. God can provide a positive mentor to come alongside us with encouragement and guidance. It's up to us to accept the help. God wants us to serve him successfully. The good news is: He's already put in place the people we need to help us get there.

So learn from your mistakes, but don't let them stop you. Use what happened in your past to positively determine what will happen in your future. Where you came from isn't nearly as important as where God is taking you. | POWER FOR LIFE BIBLE

FLYING HIGH, AUSTRALIAN CAPITAL TERRITORY, AUSTRALIA

Way beyond the balloon

"Praise be to the God and Father of our Lord Jesus Christ, who has blessed us in the heavenly realms with every spiritual blessing in Christ."

EPHESIANS 1:3

One Saturday morning, when my son, Anthony, was three years old, we were making pancakes. He started singing a song he had learned in Sunday school.

"Do, Lord, Oh Do, Lord, Oh do remember me," he sang out. "Do, Lord, Oh do, Lord, Oh do remember me."

I started teasing Anthony by singing along with him, "Do remember me... way...beyond...the red. Is that right?"

"No, Daddy. You're wrong." I kept adding colors. The more colors I added, the louder he got.

"It goes like this, silly." Anthony sang in a booming voice, "Do remember me, way beyond the balloon!"

My son may have had the words wrong, but his thoughts were right. God is waiting to bless us way beyond the balloon—and way beyond the blue, too. His blessings stretch forever, and they last forever, too!

| ROBERT A. SCHULLER

SHOSHONE FALLS, IDAHO, USA

Power outage

"I want to know Christ—yes, to know the power of his resurrection."

PHILIPPIANS 3:10

I take power for granted...until it fails. A sudden outage clarifies how many appliances need electricity. I discovered a surprising example of this when I was principal at our ministry's school.

The day began with a power failure. The staff came running, "Do we notify parents to pick up their children?"

"No. It will probably come back on soon. Window light will suffice for now."

That decision seemed right until two girls reported, "The toilets won't flush."

Toilets need electricity to flush? Five hundred kids without toilets that work?

"Call the parents immediately!" I shouted.

When you disconnect from God, Jesus, and the Holy Spirit, you suffer a power outage. It can bring discouragement, disillusionment, disappointment, and even depression. Good news: With contrition, you can plug in to God's word and prayer to restore power. | SHEILA SCHULLER COLEMAN

NIAGARA FALLS, NEW YORK, USA

Turn on God's power

"You will receive power when the Holy Spirit comes on you."

ACTS 1:8

I have two vacuum cleaners. One is a cordless that I use to clean up spills here and there. It's perfect for little jobs! But often, I have to clean up spills that are too big for the cordless. That's when I need the Dirt Devil. I have to plug this vacuum into a source of power and turn it on.

It's the same with your life. If you go through life unplugged from your source of spiritual power, pretty soon you will be out of commission. You need to stay plugged in to your source of power, the Holy Spirit, who gives you the courage and strength to face events that are unpredictable, emotions that are undependable, enthusiasm that is depleteable, and an eternity that is unattainable apart from God.

Go ahead. Turn on God's power in your life. | ROBERT A. SCHULLER

HAY BALES, SPEARVILLE, KANSAS, USA

God's promise of provision

"He provides you with plenty of food and fills your hearts with joy."

ACTS 14:17

God promises to provide for all of your needs. But it's not easy trusting for God's provision. Yes, you should be prudent. But be careful, or you'll end up like the man who was getting ready to go on a journey.

He packed his mule with basic necessities, but then thought, *What if I run into robbers? I had better take a machete.* He added the machete to the back of the mule and just as he was ready to leave, thought, *What if my mule cuts his leg? I had better take a first aid kit with me.* On and on it went until the mule was so burdened down it couldn't take a step. You get the point.

If you wait until all of your provisions are in order, you may miss out on some of life's most exciting journeys. | POWER FOR LIFE BIBLE

FROZEN PARK, NIAGARA FALLS, NEW YORK, USA

God has created you to be unique,
and designed you with everything you need to succeed in life.

ROBERT A. SCHULLER

February

DAFFODIL SUNSET, WASHINGTON, USA

Happiness formula

"Blessed are the poor in spirit, for theirs is the kingdom of heaven."

MATTHEW 5:3

People often believe they would be happy, "If only...I weren't under such financial stress...weren't sick all the time...could be successful at...could find someone to love me who..."

Even if all the "if only's" came true, they would not be guaranteed happiness. Scientists have discovered that, on average, as the level of material provision rises, the level of emotional health declines. The good news is that Jesus gave us the time-proven formula for happiness in the beatitudes, or the "Be-Happy Attitudes."

They teach us that the first principle of happiness is being willing to ask for help. When we ask for help, we are more prepared to help others, and others are more inclined to ask for help themselves. When you ask for help—you are not only helping yourself be happy—you are helping others, too!

| POWER FOR LIFE BIBLE

ST. LUKE'S ANGLICAN CHURCH, NEW SOUTH WALES, AUSTRALIA

No more blame game

"Blessed are those who mourn, for they will be comforted."

MATTHEW 5:4

Most of us have asked, "Why do bad things happen to good people?" We think if we live a good life, we will be happy, and if we live a bad life, we will be unhappy. But that is not always the case.

The better question is, "What happens to good people when bad things happen to them?" The answer Jesus gives is, "They will be comforted." He teaches us that it is possible to be happy even when sorrow casts a long, black shadow. With help, you can turn your negative into a positive, your minus into a plus, your cross into an empty tomb. It's possible to be happy anyway, if you don't blame God, yourself, or others.

You can nurse your hurt, rehearse your hurt, or reverse your hurt. It's up to you to choose healing, today! | POWER FOR LIFE BIBLE

SOLITUDE, LAKE MCDONALD, MONTANA, USA

Cool, calm, corrected

"Blessed are the meek,
for they will inherit the earth."

MATTHEW 5:5

When pushed, threatened, or mistreated, it is easy to lose our cool, spout off, or run away and retreat. It takes tremendous emotional maturity to stand our ground, coolly and calmly, and be willing to be corrected. It is not enough to be collected, we must also be willing to face our mistakes, learn from them, and grow in the process.

We must be meek—not a doormat or a martyr—but able to state our position, discuss options, admit our mistakes, accept help, and apologize. In four words, we must be:

M - Mighty, using our strength to help others.

E - Emotionally stable, even through the ups and downs.

E - Educable, continually willing to learn.

K - Kind, able to say, "It's your turn."

When you are willing to be meek, you are open to be blessed!

| POWER FOR LIFE BIBLE

SUNDRIFT GORGE, GLACIER NATIONAL PARK, MONTANA, USA

Significant hunger

"Blessed are those who hunger and thirst for righteousness,
for they will be filled."

MATTHEW 5:6

Satisfaction is a frequently futile objective. People who diet are never skinny enough, people who are rich are never rich enough, people who are successful are never successful enough. When is enough *enough?*

The never-ending, vicious cycle of striving for more can lead to a sense of dissatisfaction, unhappiness, even despair. Jesus breaks that destructive cycle by showing us that it's not the hunger for more, but the object of our hunger that is the key.

Ask yourself, "What do I hunger and thirst for?" If you seek more money, more fame, more success, or more sexual gratification, then you will likely remain frustrated. But if you have sold yourself out to a God-given dream with a purpose—if you hunger and thirst to make a significant and positive change—it is then that you will become satisfied and truly happy!

| POWER FOR LIFE BIBLE

ULURU, NORTHERN TERRITORY, AUSTRALIA

The forgiveness question

"Blessed are the merciful, for they will be shown mercy."

MATTHEW 5:7

There may be no other topic that people resist more than the topic of forgiveness.

It is likely that there will be multiple times in your life when people will hurt you terribly and they will never apologize for what they have done. Then, what? Do you hold a grudge for the rest of your life? Unfortunately that attitude will result in isolation and loneliness, not to mention the possibility of high blood pressure, a stroke, heart trouble, even cancer—all caused by the stress that accompanies such a negative response.

Is it worth the risk? Remember that forgiveness is more for you than for the one you are forgiving.

To forgive or not forgive—that is the question. One leads to health and happiness, the other to allowing the hurt to live on and keep on hurting. Which will you choose? | POWER FOR LIFE BIBLE

CRADLE MOUNTAIN, TASMANIA, AUSTRALIA

Fearless faith

"Blessed are the pure in heart, for they will see God."

MATTHEW 5:8

Corrie Ten Boom, the founder of a powerful ministry, was the sole survivor of a Protestant Dutch family that had been incarcerated in concentration camps for hiding Jews in their home. During many lectures, Corrie would share a precious childhood memory of her father responding to her fear that she didn't have enough faith. He asked, "Corrie, when we take a trip on the train, do I give you the ticket a year, a month, even a day before you need it?"

"No, Papa...because I might lose it?"

"No, it's because you don't need it then. I wait until you need it."

So it is with our faith in God. He waits until we need it to give it to us. But when we need it, do not fear. He will supply all that you need—especially your need to have faith. | POWER FOR LIFE BIBLE

YANKEE BOY BASIN, COLORADO, USA

The planks of peace

"Blessed are the peacemakers,
for they will be called children of God."

MATTHEW 5:9

Where God sees a breach between people, he builds a bridge. And he uses his children to help with the construction. God calls us to be peacemakers, building bridges across chasms separating individuals or groups, providing a common plank of understanding across which we can walk together.

Needless to say, Jesus Christ was the ultimate peacemaker. He laid down his life to build a bridge—between God and us, and between us and our fellow man. The cross of Jesus is the supreme symbol of a perfect bridge. The vertical plank connects us to God and the horizontal plank connects us to our neighbors.

In times of conflict, think of the cross and its high cost, lovingly paid. If you serve the cause of peace on the bridge of the cross, your efforts will not be in vain | POWER FOR LIFE BIBLE

LOWER TAHQUAMENON FALLS, MICHIGAN, USA

Frustration to freedom

*"Blessed are those who are persecuted because of righteousness,
for theirs is the kingdom of heaven."*

MATTHEW 5:10

Victor Frankl, author of *Man's Search for Meaning*, conceived of his pioneering logotherapy while in a concentration camp during the Holocaust. When they took away his clothes and finally his wedding band, this thought came to him: "You can take away my belongings, you can take away my freedom, but you can *never* take away my freedom to react to what you do to me!"

When faced with persecution, we still have the freedom to choose how we will react. We can react with depression, even thoughts of suicide, or we can react by asking, "What can we learn from this? How can we turn this into something beautiful for God?"

Blessed are those who can see meaning in life and purpose in all things, for they are comforted knowing that God's hand is at work—even in the most distressing circumstances. | POWER FOR LIFE BIBLE

MATANUSKA GLACIER, ALASKA, USA

God can change a heart

"Love the Lord your God, listen to his voice, and hold fast to him."

DEUTERONOMY 30:20

I know a man who used to hate anyone who was different from him—especially blacks and Jews. In fact, he hated them so much that he kept a gun tucked under the front seat of his car and went out looking for opportunities to use it.

Eventually his violence landed him in prison. And it was there that he began reading the Bible. The more he read it, the more God's love penetrated his heart. He yielded his pent-up hatred to God and asked the Lord to change him.

Today this man, Tom Tarrants, is a loving, soft-spoken person. God's love radiates from him. He pastors a racially mixed inner-city church and works tirelessly on issues related to racial harmony.

God alone changes hearts. And his love and power can flow through anyone who is yielded to him. | ROBERT A. SCHULLER

ATCHAFALAYA SWAMP, LOUISIANA, USA

Beauty of the ordinary

"A poor widow came and put in two very small copper coins,
worth only a fraction of a penny. Jesus said,
'Truly this woman has put more into the treasury than all the others.'"

MARK 12:42-43

William Wolcott, a great English artist, went to New York City in 1924 to record his impressions of the city's architecture. One morning he found himself in the architectural office of a colleague for whom he'd worked years before. Suddenly he had an urge to sketch and said to his colleague, "Please, I need some paper." Seeing some paper on the desk, Wolcott asked if he could have it. His colleague replied, "That's not sketching paper, Mr. Wolcott—that's just ordinary wrapping paper." Not wanting to lose the inspiration of the moment, Wolcott picked up the paper and said, "Nothing is ordinary if you know how to use it." He took the paper and on it drew two sketches. One sold for $1,000, the other for $500.

We can take the "castaways" of life and from them create something new and beautiful. | ROBERT H. SCHULLER

ALLEY SPRING, MISSOURI, USA

God is blessing you now

*"May you be richly rewarded by the Lord, the God of Israel,
under whose wings you have come to take refuge."*

RUTH 2:12

It's not always easy to see the blessings of God as they unfold.

Are you going through a tough time? Do you sometimes find yourself wondering what happened—how you got to this awful point in your life? Perhaps you find yourself looking back on "the good ol' days" that were filled with promise and hope, and wondering exactly where it was that things went wrong.

Maybe financial problems are crowding in on you. Perhaps you've lost someone you loved. Maybe you're sick and in continuous pain. Or maybe you're just tired of fighting your way upstream against a raging current.

I don't know how hurt you feel, how frustrated you are, or how the actions of others have damaged you. But I do know one thing: Whatever is happening in your life, God is there, and he is blessing you now! | ROBERT A. SCHULLER

SUNFLOWERS, NEW SOUTH WALES, AUSTRALIA

God's love can never be lost

"God is love."

1 JOHN 4:8

Have you ever lost something you treasured? Remember the sick feeling you had thinking you would never see it again? What treasure would guarantee you heartbreak if you lost it? What would you be willing to do to replace it? Maybe it's the diamond in your engagement ring, or a photo of your parents.

Whatever it is—it is nothing compared to the love of Christ. Can you imagine losing his love? Actually, maybe you think you can or have lost his love because of something you did or failed to do. Maybe you fear you lost his love because you didn't spend enough time praying or worshiping God. Or maybe you think you lost his love because you haven't gone to church lately.

The truth is: You can never earn God's love—nor can you ever lose it. What a blessed assurance! | SHEILA SCHULLER COLEMAN

VICTORIA FALLS, ZIMBABWE

Positively shocking love

"Give thanks to the Lord, for he is good; his love endures forever."

1 CHRONICLES 16:34

I loved sitting in Dad's lap after dinner when he sank into his favorite easy chair. One night I noticed a light bulb was missing from the adjacent pole lamp used for reading. Out of curiosity I stuck my finger into the empty socket.

Dad yelped and jumped up, nearly dumping me onto the floor.

"Sheila, why did you do that?"

"I didn't know it would hurt."

My curiosity hurt both of us. The electric current flowed from the socket through my finger to my dad.

How often has your curiosity hurt not only you, but also your earthly father and even your Heavenly Father? In truth, when you hurt, God hurts. It is impossible to make a hurtful mistake without hurting others.

God's love is shocking in power and endurance. Nothing can separate you from your Heavenly Father. That is positively shocking!

| SHEILA SCHULLER COLEMAN

THE SKILLION, TERRIGAL, NEW SOUTH WALES, AUSTRALIA

The security of God's love

"I am the Lord; those who hope in me will not be disappointed."

ISAIAH 49:23

When I was in college, a friend of mine wanted to date a girl on campus who he thought was the most beautiful girl he had ever seen. Not only did my friend get a date with her, he fell in love with her and married her. They came close to making it into *Guinness World Records* as one of the shortest and unhappiest marriages on record.

If you're looking for other people to save you from the storms of life, you're looking in the wrong place. The greatest people in the world are, after everything is said and done, only people, and that means they are capable of failing you.

God, on the other hand, will never let you down. He will never turn his back on you. Unlike human love, God's love is all-consuming and does not change. | ROBERT A. SCHULLER

SWIFT CURRENT FALLS, GLACIER NATIONAL PARK, MONTANA, USA

Love that liberates

"For God so loved the world that he gave his one and only Son, that whoever believes in him shall not perish but have eternal life."

JOHN 3:16

I grew up on a farm in Iowa. Every spring my father would get thousands of baby chicks. He raised them to become laying hens. Then he sold their eggs. Those baby chicks were the softest, cutest little creatures imaginable. But as a young boy my father would frequently have to remind me, "Bob, don't hold them so tight. You'll suffocate them." To which I'd reply, "But I love them so much!"

"If you love them," he would say, "let them go."

I had to be reminded of that when my first child turned eighteen, when my second child graduated from high school...as well as my third, fourth, and fifth.

Letting go of someone you love is never easy. But unless you let go, they will never grow into mature adults. Real love liberates. That's what faith teaches and what Christ demonstrated. | ROBERT H. SCHULLER

VIEW FROM HUNT'S MESA, MONUMENT VALLEY, ARIZONA, USA

Simple truths

*"Trust in the Lord with all your heart
and lean not on your own understanding."*

PROVERBS 3:5

I'll never forget the story of the young boy who went to Sunday school and was taught that we're all made in the image of God. He also learned that God created the first man from the dust of the earth and that when we die the body once more turns to dust.

One evening as the little boy knelt by his bed to say his prayers, he suddenly stiffened with fear. His mother asked, "Tommy, what's wrong?" Looking under the bed he sneezed from the dust accumulated there and said, "There are hundreds of them under the bed. I just can't tell if they're coming or going!"

Dust to dust. It's tempting to make God's word more complex than he ever intended. His truths are simple. They are redeeming. They give us God's timeless design for divine dignity. | ROBERT H. SCHULLER

CHRIST CHURCH, ST. SIMONS ISLAND, GEORGIA, USA

Your second family

"No one has ever seen God; but if we love one another,
God lives in us and his love is made complete in us."

1 JOHN 4:12

In January 1984, I announced to my church congregation that I was soon to experience a divorce from my wife. I had no idea how the congregation would respond. After finishing my remarks I sat down, bowed my head, and sat staring at the floor.

Within seconds I heard the sound of footsteps coming toward me. I looked up to discover that nearly the entire congregation had joined me on the platform. They came to affirm their love for me and to assure me my ministry was not over. My church family held me up during what was one of the most difficult moments of my life as a person and as a pastor. Their strength convinced me I could survive.

What difficulty are you facing today? Lean on one of God's greatest gifts to you—the church, your second family. | ROBERT A. SCHULLER

TULIPS, TASMANIA, AUSTRALIA

Be a hope-a-holic

"Be joyful in hope."

ROMANS 12:12

When asked, at the end of his career, what great lessons he had learned from history, the great American historian Charles Beard answered, "I've learned four: First—whom the gods would destroy, they first make mad with power. Second—the mills of God grind slowly, yet they grind exceedingly fine. Third—the bee fertilizes the flower it robs. Fourth—only when it's dark are you able to see the stars."

Charles Beard was a *hope-a-holic*. So am I. I have an incurable, instinctive, impulsive tendency to surrender to hope. I know yesterday is a cancelled check. Today is cash in hand to spend as I want. And tomorrow is a promissory note from God Almighty.

This hope will not disappoint. Our "hopes" may not all be fulfilled, but hope is its own immediate reward; it offers us the gift of unceasing optimism.

| ROBERT H. SCHULLER

ULURU SILHOUETTE, AUSTRALIA

Name above all names

"Therefore God...gave him the name that is above every name."

PHILIPPIANS 2:9

Californians tend to be very fashion-conscious. And I'll admit that on occasion, I've browsed in some of the stores on Rodeo Drive in Beverly Hills. Where else can you find a small pocketbook on sale for $600 and a shirt or blouse for even more? Why are they so expensive? Because of the names attached to them. Admittedly in such cases, those names stand for quality, good workmanship, and status.

People everywhere want to wear Gucci ties or Bill Blass coats, or dresses bearing the name of Liz Claiborne or Anne Klein. And kids insist on wearing Michael Jordan or Shaquille O'Neil shoes. The *only* thing that makes one article of clothing more expensive or more highly regarded than another is the name attached to it.

There is value attached to the right name. Remember, you have God's name attached to you. | ROBERT A. SCHULLER

OUTBACK ROAD, SOUTH AUSTRALIA, AUSTRALIA

Positive expectations

"Run with perseverance the race marked out."

HEBREWS 12:1

Have you ever stood at the starting line of a race? Have you ever stood at the foot of a mountain? Have you ever stood at the back of a church to walk down the aisle poised and eager to begin a new life in marriage?

What did you feel? Was your heart racing with excitement? Was there positive anticipation? Your positive expectations provide the powerful thrust needed to launch you into something new.

Take a moment to capture the excitement you feel today. Record it in a journal. Then, the positive force of diving into a new endeavor can be available for harnessing and you can tap into it whenever obstacles occur further down the course. God calls you to run the race well in order to make it across the finish line successfully. | SHEILA SCHULLER COLEMAN

WHITE SANDS NATIONAL MONUMENT, NEW MEXICO, USA

The power of a positive attitude

"When Jesus heard this, he was astonished and said,
'I tell you the truth, I have not found anyone in Israel with such great faith.'"

MATTHEW 8:10

Nothing generates as much energy, enthusiasm, or vitality in life as a positive mental attitude.

I'm reminded of the story of a little boy who was overheard talking to himself as he strutted through the backyard, baseball cap in place, toting a bat and ball. "I'm the greatest batter in the world," he said proudly. He tossed the ball into the air, swung at it, and missed. Undaunted, he picked up the ball, threw it into the air, and said to himself as he swung at the ball again, "I am the greatest batter ever!" But again he missed. He paused a moment, then threw the ball into the air again and shouted, "I'm the greatest baseball batter who ever lived!" He swung hard but missed again. "Wow!" he exclaimed, "What a great pitcher!"

Now that's a positive mental attitude! | ROBERT H. SCHULLER

SUNRISE, BETHANY BEACH, DELAWARE, USA

Yes. Wait. No.

"I call on you, my God, for you will answer me;
turn your ear to me and hear my prayer."

PSALM 17:6

Sometimes we pray and immediately see God's hand move in a positive response to our prayers...and we know that he is alive and cares about us. But then there are times when what we ask for doesn't come, and we don't understand why God isn't giving us what we believe is so critically important. In his wisdom, God knows that we need to grow and that we're not prepared to receive what we're asking for.

Sometimes God answers our prayers by saying no. I can't tell you why he says no. Sometimes it doesn't seem fair...but then, we can't see things from his vantage point so we have to release our own desires. When we do, his peace floods our soul.

When you pray, give God control of your life—it's the most important thing you can do. | ROBERT A. SCHULLER

HARDY REEF, GREAT BARRIER REEF, QUEENSLAND, AUSTRALIA

Hidden treasures

"It is the glory of God to conceal a thing.
And it is the glory of kings to search things out."

PROVERBS 25:2

The greatest, most valuable treasures are rarely in plain view. The pearl is hidden within the oyster, beneath the deep waters of the ocean. The diamond is buried below the earth's surface. And gold nuggets are concealed within huge icebergs and inside mountains.

It is the glory of God to conceal a good thing. I firmly believe that the solutions to our biggest global problems—energy, economics and natural resources—are planted by God within the universe. They lie beneath the sea, within the earth, or in the distant heavens because God has hidden them there.

But the greatest of God's treasures are found within you and me—the treasures of human creativity and potential! We are gems of incredible value, pearls of great price. God has concealed them within us. It's up to us to uncover them. | ROBERT H. SCHULLER

RUSSELL FALLS, TASMANIA, AUSTRALIA

Arrow prayers

"Whatever you ask in my name the Father will give you."

JOHN 15:16

A teacher at a Christian school heard sirens in the distance. "Quick, children!" she instructed, "fold your hands and send up an arrow prayer." She led the children in a prayer for the paramedics who were racing to the scene and for the people who had been in the accident.

When the children went home, they told their parents about their experience in class that day. Now every time they hear a siren, the children send up arrow prayers wherever they are—in a restaurant, in the car, or at home.

God's answer is just an arrow prayer away. He's always on call.

"Help, Lord! I'm feeling discouraged!"

"Help, Lord! I'm feeling afraid!"

"Help, Lord, I feel like I'm drowning!"

Then, wait and watch—he'll be the first on the scene!

| SHEILA SCHULLER COLEMAN

SUNRISE, LAKE ERIE, OHIO, USA

Morning exercise

"In the morning, Lord, I lay my requests before you and wait expectantly."

PSALM 5:3

I'll be honest—I have a tough time getting started in the morning—at least until I've had my first cup of coffee.

One day a friend shared with me a little technique he uses to jump-start his day. He told me, "When you get up in the morning, clap your hands... then rub them together." I did as he suggested, adding my own little spin to the exercise.

Here's what I do: I get up, clap my hands, rub them together and say, "Thank you, God, for this great new day. You've given me one more day to worship and live for you. Help me to make the most of this wonderful opportunity."

Why don't you try it right now? All done? Now you're ready to go out and enjoy this wonderful day the Lord has given you! | ROBERT A. SCHULLER

SNAKE RIVER, GRAND TETON NATIONAL PARK, WYOMING, USA

Slow and steady

"My heart, O God, is steadfast, my heart is steadfast."

PSALM 57:7

Every New Year's Day I sit down and write out a list of my goals for the year. I keep that list in a place where I can check it from time to time to make sure I'm heading in the right direction. But I understand that I'm not going to achieve everything on that list overnight.

I also have a list of more immediate things to do that I keep with me all the time. Sometimes my list gets very long. That's okay because I don't let that list run my life. Instead, I use it to keep myself organized and on track. I now understand that old fable about the tortoise and the hare—"slow and steady wins the race."

Pace yourself. Take your time. And you'll see, experience, smell, taste, touch, and enjoy things that you would otherwise miss.

| ROBERT A. SCHULLER

WHEAT FIELDS, BLAINE, IDAHO, USA

Harmony seekers

*"Peacemakers who sow in peace
reap a harvest of righteousness."*

JAMES 3:18

I innately seek harmony and avoid conflict. So, what was God thinking when he gave me four sons who fought constantly? Or when he put me in a career requiring conflict resolution ninety percent of the time?

I learned the hard way that harmony seekers are often the best at conflict resolution because we're highly motivated to settle conflicts quickly.

As an administrator, I've also discovered that good, healthy conflict can stimulate better team creativity and results. Still...I side-step conflict, whenever I can. If I can't, then I face it with gratitude for the challenging lessons to be learned through it.

I am a peacemaker. What I've learned from Jesus is that peace comes at a price and with supreme sacrifice. Jesus, the Prince of Peace, walks every step with me in times of conflict and in peace. | SHEILA SCHULLER COLEMAN

AMISH COUNTRY, LANCASTER, PENNSYLVANIA, USA

God's good plans!

"'For I know the plans I have for you,' declares the Lord,
'plans to prosper you and not to harm you, plans to give you hope and a future.'"

JEREMIAH 29:11

Plans—we write them. God rights them!

Our best-laid plans run into unforeseen challenges and obstacles from time to time. Even with the finest minds, mistakes can be made. There is no such thing as a fool-proof plan.

But, who of us would worry, knowing that an expert had his hand on the wheel of our life? Would we try to wrestle it away like a child demanding his or her own way, even though it might lead to destruction? Or would we welcome it, feel the wind blow through our hair, and enjoy the ride knowing we're in good hands?

God loves it when we trust him—when we lean back and enjoy the ride. He loves it when we write our plans prayerfully, but allow him to right our plans and lead us to the blessings he has in store for us. | POWER FOR LIFE BIBLE

BLACKEYED SUSAN, IOWA, USA

Say yes to abundant living

"I have come that they may have life, and have it to the full."

JOHN 10:10

Boundaries—we are all encouraged to set boundaries and to learn how to say no. But there is far more that can be lost by saying no, than by saying yes.

Say yes to the Lord's dream for your life.

Say yes to the Lord's call on your life.

Say yes to believing in God's love.

Say yes to giving your life to Jesus.

Will you risk being too busy? Perhaps. Will you risk feeling overwhelmed at times? Probably. But, you can either miss the adventure or you can live life abundantly. It's your choice. In the words of a familiar old quote: "Only one life, 'twill soon be past. Only what's done for Christ will last!"

Say yes to living life abundantly! | SHEILA SCHULLER COLEMAN

UNCOMPAHGRE NATIONAL FOREST, COLORADO, USA

*Tune in to God
and tune in on life.*

ROBERT H. SCHULLER

March

MOONEY FALLS, SUPAI, ARIZONA, USA

It's not all up to you

"God's love has been poured out into our hearts through the Holy Spirit, who has been given to us."

ROMANS 5:5

You cannot develop a loving attitude all by yourself. No, love is a supernatural gift from God, one of the fruits of the Spirit. That doesn't mean there isn't anything you can do to cultivate that fruit. It's important to be yielded to the Holy Spirit.

Sometimes you block what God wants to do in your life by holding on to negative attitudes or stubbornly refusing to change even though you know he wants you to. You say, "Oh, come on, God, you can't expect me to love that guy. You don't know what he's done to me." But God *does* know...and he calls you to love that person anyway.

It's not up to you to single-handedly change your life. It is up to you to let God work in you to help you become the loving person he wants you to be.

| ROBERT A. SCHULLER

TERRIGAL BEACH, NEW SOUTH WALES, AUSTRALIA

Creativity's true source

"I will tell you of new things,
of hidden things unknown to you."

ISAIAH 48:6

Is there anything new under the sun? Has every original thought already been conceived? The only true original is Almighty God—Creator of all life and all ideas.

So, how can you be a creator of something fresh and new? How do you come up with an idea that no one else has thought of?

First, spend time looking at what others are doing. Some people are afraid to do research for fear of being influenced and their creativity being adversely diminished as a result of it. But all fresh ideas are just old ideas with a new twist. Once you've spent time looking into existing creations, tap into the ultimate source of creative power, plug into your Creator. The closer you are to him, the more creative and fresh your ideas will be. His supply is endless. Tap into the Creator today. | SHEILA SCHULLER COLEMAN

OXBOW BEND, GRAND TETON NATIONAL PARK, WYOMING, USA

Are you drifting downstream?

*"You will seek me and find me
when you seek me with all your heart."*

JEREMIAH 29:13

Novelist Leo Tolstoy tells the parable of a man who was given a boat and two oars and told to row to the opposite shore. As he was rowing he suddenly found himself in the middle of the river surrounded by boats filled with laughing people. They were drifting along, not a care in the world. "Is this the right way?" he inquired.

"What other way is there?" they quipped.

Soon he was drifting downstream with them. Then he heard a roar in the distance. It was the rapids and a waterfall. He picked up the oars, rowed as hard as he could, and finally broke free of the forceful pull of the current and crowd.

Are you drifting downstream with the crowd? Are you caught in the current? Pick up the oars. Go the other direction. God will save you.

| ROBERT H. SCHULLER

BYRON BAY LIGHTHOUSE, NEW SOUTH WALES, AUSTRALIA

Wahoo

*"The lot is cast into the lap,
but its every decision is from the Lord.*

PROVERBS 16:33

A favorite Schuller-kid game was Wahoo, a board drilled with holes. Marbles sitting in holes were moved by dice roll.

One mountain vacation, Dad decided to play the game with us. He had just about won when one lucky roll knocked his marble back to the start. "That's it!" Dad declared. "I'm driving to town to get another game—one that's not just sheer luck."

Driving dark mountain roads, he returned in an hour jubilantly carrying a new game. Poor Dad! Upon pouring over the rules, we discovered he had purchased Parcheesi, a replicate of Wahoo!

It's tempting to trade one trial, career, or job for another thinking it's better, only to discover the replacement isn't any better, or, maddeningly, is even worse. Stop and pray before jumping ship. Ask God to guide you or to redeem a bad decision before it's too late. | SHEILA SCHULLER COLEMAN

WHITE SANDS NATIONAL MONUMENT, NEW MEXICO, USA

Jesus calls, "Follow me."

*"Then Jesus said...'Whoever wants to be my disciple
must deny themselves and take up their cross and follow me.'"*

MATTHEW 16:24

Who of us likes to pay taxes? Taxes are nothing new, and tax collector have been unpopular for centuries. Matthew was a tax collector whose profits came from the excess he could squeeze from people. His profession offered him the fastest, surest route to making money in Galilee.

When Jesus called Matthew to become one of his twelve apostles, he was sending the message that he can use anyone! For Matthew, following Jesus meant leaving behind substantial wealth. Yet he did not hesitate for a moment to answer yes when Jesus called, "Follow me."

If Jesus could find such a lofty place for a misfit such as Matthew, he can find a place for you and me. So open your heart. Listen with your soul. And you'll hear Jesus say, "Follow me." | POWER FOR LIFE BIBLE

MONA VALE, NEW SOUTH WALES, AUSTRALIA

Disconnected by disappointment?

"Those who hope in me will not be disappointed."

ISAIAH 49:23

What do you do when your life doesn't turn out the way you hoped it would? What happens to your relationship with God when your prayers fail to bring the answers you asked for? How do you keep on believing when you see others get their miracle—only to have your miracle denied? Disappointments such as these can rupture your relationship with God and shatter your faith.

Yet, God frequently demonstrates his blessing by redirecting you from what you think is best for your life—to what he *knows* is best for your life. Rather than withholding blessings—in truth, he is steering you away from pain and closer to him. Though you can't see it today, trust that he will make the blessings crystal clear in days to come. | SHEILA SCHULLER COLEMAN

ANDROSCOGGIN RIVER, MAINE, USA

The master's touch

"He has made everything beautiful in its time."

ECCLESIASTES 3:11

An orchestra had one of the best first-chair violinists ever. Word got out that he had purchased a new Stradivarius, the finest violin made. The night of the concert, the theatre was packed. The music began and with each crescendo, the audience's emotions swelled. They were overcome by the beauty of the sound.

At the end of the concert, the violinist stood, raised his violin, and as the audience applauded wildly, he broke his violin over his knee. The audience stood in stunned silence.

Holding the mangled instrument in his hand, the violinist said, "This violin did not make the music. I bought it at a pawn shop for $150." Then he added, "It's the *master* who makes the music."

It doesn't matter what failures or successes you've had—it's the Master who makes beautiful music through you! | ROBERT A. SCHULLER

LOTUS FLOWERS, MISSISSIPPI, USA

A family of faith

"All were one in heart and mind…
And God's grace was so powerfully at work in them all."

ACTS 4:32-33

As firstborn of the Schuller children, I'm enough older than Carol and Gretchen to be their "para-mom." One summer, our parents were in Korea for a conference and my sisters were visiting family in Iowa. I had remained in California to work. I was newly engaged. My sisters couldn't wait to see my ring.

But the night before I was to pick them up at the airport, a call came: "Carol's been in a motorcycle accident and is in surgery. They can't save her leg."

Schullers convened at Carol's bedside from around the world. We held each other, prayed, and shared Scripture to find desperately needed strength, thankful that Carol had lost her leg, not her life!

These were some of the most difficult days we ever faced. But we got through them together—a family of faith, holding each other up.

| SHEILA SCHULLER COLEMAN

SNOWDRIFT, CRADLE MOUNTAIN, TASMANIA, AUSTRALIA

Dare to say yes

"And by faith even Sarah, who was past childbearing age, was enabled to bear children because she considered him faithful who had made the promise."

HEBREWS 11:11

Has anyone ever said to you, "You would be excellent at...."? You know it's true, but it seems beyond your reach. You believe God can do anything, but *that*? No, *that's* impossible!

God challenges you as he did Sarah, "Is anything too hard for me?" His dream might seem impossible, but the fact that it can only be done with God's help is evidence that it is God's dream. We can do the possible all by ourselves—the impossible requires God's intervention.

Faith enables us to say yes to God even when our life experience warns us to say no. Faith confronts the doubts, the fears, the improbabilities, and embraces the truth that with God all things are possible! Sarah laughed at God, but God saw a hint of faith mixed with her doubts. Believe in the impossible. Nothing is too hard for God! | POWER FOR LIFE BIBLE

SECOND BEACH, OLYMPIC NATIONAL PARK, WYOMING, USA

Keep on believing

*"He has reconciled you...to present you holy in his sight...
if you continue in your faith."*

COLOSSIANS 1:22-23

Where is God when you can't see or feel him? Has he deserted you? Does he only help those who have more faith? Such questions erode your faith at times when you need it the most. The truth is: God's love and power remain unlimited. He can help every person simultaneously.

How, then, can you keep on believing when you can't see God? You can find encouragement from the faith of survivors of the Holocaust who kept on believing even when their faith was sorely challenged. Anne Frank wrote in her diary, "I still believe that people are good at heart." On the wall of a hiding place was scrawled this poem, "I believe in the sun even when it is not shining. I believe in love even when I can't feel it. I believe in God, even when he is silent." | SHEILA SCHULLER COLEMAN

REFLECTIONS, WILLIAMSVILLE, VERMONT, USA

Example of faithfulness

"Abraham believed God, and it was credited to him as righteousness, and he was called God's friend."

JAMES 2:23

What comes to mind when you think of *faithfulness*? Do you think of being "full of faith" or being "trustworthy and reliable"? Faithfulness is both.

God gives us a certain amount of faith, but our faith grows through a continual process of trusting him. Abraham of the Old Testament is one of the best examples of this type of faith. He never doubted that God would fulfill his promise to make him a father of many nations.

Faith was a constant in Abraham's life. His first steps of faith led to more faith until even the most startling command from God—to sacrifice his only son Isaac—allowed him to respond obediently without losing confidence in God.

We must learn to do the same. When we understand that God is totally trustworthy, even the most difficult steps of obedience become possible.

| ROBERT A. SCHULLER

BIG RED, QUEENSLAND, AUSTRALIA

A blessed life

"The Lord Jesus himself said:
'It is more blessed to give than to receive.'"

ACTS 20:35

My mother was a blessed woman. The key to her happiness was her giving nature. She habitually gave back to the Lord ten percent of her money. Not only did she give of her meager income, but she also gave of herself. For my mother that meant apple pies. I can still picture her in the kitchen, slicing the apples, piling them high in the deep pie pan, and sprinkling cinnamon, butter, and sugar on top. Then she would wrap the crust over the mile-high pile of apples, sealing it carefully.

Her pies were a work of art, and she never made just one of them. She always made two—one for us and one for somebody in town who could "use" a pie. Mom was her happiest when doing kind things for others.

Learn to give and your life will be blessed. | ROBERT H. SCHULLER

OMEO VALLEY, VICTORIA, AUSTRALIA

Stop for directions

"He guides the humble in what is right and teaches them his way."

PSALM 25:9

The Israelites had to cross the wilderness to get to the Promised Land. Since none of them knew the way and there was no guide available or landmarks to provide direction, the people had no choice but to completely rely on God to show them the way. He led them by providing a pillar of clouds by day and fire by night.

God doesn't lead in such conspicuous ways today, but he still guides. STOP! Make a timeline of your life, identifying five pivotal points where your life took a turn. Then answer these questions: How did God guide you through those times? How was he there for you? If you got off track, what did God use to get you back on course?

God wants to guide you as clearly as he did the Israelites. Ask him to.

| POWER FOR LIFE BIBLE

SUNFLOWER SUNRISE, GOODLAND, KANSAS, USA

Songs of faith

"Is anyone happy? Let them sing songs of praise."

JAMES 5:13

My mother has always said, "Be careful what songs you teach to children. Once they learn a song, the words will be a part of them forever."

I was especially enriched as a child. Choir rehearsals were held in our home. Hearing music wafting through my bedroom, I would creep quietly past chairs set up for the choir members to squeeze behind the couch where I could listen.

Alas, inevitably I would feel Mom tugging on my leg to shoo me back to bed. But even from under my covers, I could hear great hymns of faith praising God, such as,

Great is Thy faithfulness!
Morning by morning new mercies I see.
All I have needed Thy hand hath provided;
Great is Thy faithfulness, Lord, unto me!

Thank you, Lord, for songs of faith that filled my life!

| SHEILA SCHULLER COLEMAN

EAST ORANGE, VERMONT, USA

Do the math

"He determines the number of the stars and calls them each by name."

PSALM 147:4

When my kids were young, I would have fun with them doing math equations. They loved it because they could always get the right answer...as long as I multiplied by zero. I would ask them, "What's five times zero?" And they'd answer, "Zero!"

"What's 285 times zero?" I'd ask. "Zero!" they'd yell.

Finally, I'd tell them, "Now I'm going to give you the hardest equation ever—what's 854,356,484 times zero?" ...I could never trick my children. They learned very quickly that multiplying zero by whatever you have, still gives you zero!

But multiply one times God and what do you get? Multiply a fraction of anything you have by God and you can't even count the number! When we try to do things in our own ability, it's a tough equation. But anything multiplied by God works. | ROBERT A. SCHULLER

TERRIGAL SUNRISE, NEW SOUTH WALES, AUSTRALIA

Find strength in joy

"The joy of the Lord is your strength."

NEHEMIAH 8:10

I knew a man who exuded joy. It didn't matter what was going on in his life, the joy was always there. Certainly he wasn't always happy. He had his share of difficulties. But even during the worst of times, this man was joyful. You could see the joy in his eyes.

Happiness, by way of contrast, is often dependent on circumstances and frequently fleeting. It's what you feel when your boss tells you he's giving you a raise. Or when your favorite team makes it to the World Series or Super Bowl.

The kind of joy God wants you to have—the joy his Spirit gives—is not dependent on your circumstances. It is the confident assurance that God loves you and is at work in your life and will be there for you no matter happens. | ROBERT A. SCHULLER

CATHEDRAL ROCKS, NEW SOUTH WALES, AUSTRALIA

Rainbow of promise

"I have set my rainbow in the clouds,
and it will be the sign of the covenant between me and the earth."

GENESIS 9:13

The story of Noah and the ark is one of promise. God's people turned their backs on God, but he reached out to Noah and his family to preserve a remnant of his creation. Noah honored God's call, and in doing so, saved his family and himself from utter destruction from a flood. As a symbol of his promise never to cover the earth again with a flood, God set a rainbow in the sky.

Next time you see a rainbow remember that God always keeps his promises. But you don't have to see a rainbow to know and rest on that assurance. God is a God of positive promises. He has promised never to leave you or forsake you and that you can have an *abundant* life.

Claim his promises today and believe in them! You have nothing to lose and everything to gain! | POWER FOR LIFE BIBLE

DESERT NEAR RED ROCK CANYON, NEVADA, USA

The heat is on

"Cast your cares on the Lord and he will sustain you."

PSALM 55:22

Potters usually glaze their work. Glazes provide the colors to pottery, but when they are applied to the clay, the colors are very muddy and hard to discern. This makes the entire process of glazing pottery difficult. It is not until the pottery is fired in a kiln of 1,000 degrees to 1,200 degrees C that the glaze begins to show its true colors. The intense heat melts the glaze, creating a type of colored-glass coating. This process is what makes the pottery not only beautiful but also durable, even though still breakable.

Similarly, when we are in the furnace of life's trials and allow God to be in there with us when the heat is on, then our true colors will shine. The hotter life gets, the more we can see, feel, and appreciate God's power.

| POWER FOR LIFE BIBLE

THE STORE, SOUTH AUSTRALIA, AUSTRALIA

Not junk, but treasure

"He chose us in him before the creation of the world
to be holy and blameless in his sight."

EPHESIANS 1:4

Dad's brother, Henry, lived on the family homestead in Iowa. We loved spending time there, where, out in a large field ditch, neighbors would dump their old junk. We children loved digging through it for broken toys, pots, pans, baskets, even costume jewelry. Uncle Henry and Aunt Alberta probably shuddered when we inevitably dragged stuff back to the farmhouse. One time we found a trove of copper pots we recycled for cash, and a jewelry box of rings perfect for young girls playing dress-up. Grandpa (Anthony Schuller) rescued, lovingly cleaned, and repaired most of the toys visiting children played with.

I've often thought how God never sees you or me as junk. He sees the potential, the treasure hidden within. He looks beyond our banged up, bruised souls to the beauties we are when we let him redeem, rescue, and restore us. | SHEILA SCHULLER COLEMAN

SUNRISE OVER THE SEA OF GALILEE, ISRAEL

Heaven signals the hurting

"God did this so that they would seek him and perhaps reach out for him and find him, though he is not far from any one of us."

ACTS 17:27

Where is God when we're hurting? How can we possibly believe that he loves us when we are going through such painful times?

In many marvelous and wonderful ways God signals us when we're suffering in spirit. It may be through a flower that's blooming or in a bird's song. Or we may see a toddler running and laughing or hear a melody we haven't heard for years. We may feel the touch of sunlight on our cheeks or see its reflection in drops of water on the leaves.

God is alive. Alert. Energetic. He's on the move, sending positive signals of life into our thoughts. It's the ultimate, healing, human experience—God's Spirit signaling us in times of need.

God's signals will come from strange and even foreign faces and places. Be prepared to accept the signals heaven is sending your way.

ROBERT H. SCHULLER

KAKADU, NORTHERN TERRITORY, AUSTRALIA

Inspired inklings

"For the Spirit God gave us does not make us timid,
but gives us power, love and self-discipline."

2 TIMOTHY 1:7

If you can discover your calling, the purpose God designed you to fulfill you will find enthusiasm. Conversely, if you are plagued with apathy, a lack of purpose, a sense of "what's the point of it all?" you will miss out on the joy and excitement that come from being enthusiastic.

Chances are you have had inklings of what it is you are supposed to be doing. You have felt godly nudges to follow a path, to tackle a dream, to take a risky stand, but perhaps fear of failure held you back. If that is your story then try to dream again. This time, dream your dream based on God's power rather than your own. God is the true source of energy that is manifested as enthusiasm. | POWER FOR LIFE BIBLE

BLUE RIDGE PARKWAY, NORTH CAROLINA, USA

My friend Jesus

"But as for me, it is good to be near God.
I have made the sovereign Lord my refuge."

PSALM 73:28

Playing piano in Grandma's parlor was a favorite pastime. I spent hours reading old hymn stories. One of my favorites was "What a Friend We Have in Jesus." Joseph Scriven wrote the words to that hymn, in 1855, to comfort his mother. His own life was beset with grief after losing two fiancés to illness and death. Despite his grief, he knew where to turn when life overwhelmed him. His legacy of faith continues to strengthen many today:

What a Friend we have in Jesus, all our sins and griefs to bear!
What a privilege to carry everything to God in prayer!
O what peace we often forfeit, O what needless pain we bear,
All because we do not carry everything to God in prayer.

This song remains in my spiritual memory. What a privilege—my friend Jesus is only a prayer away. | SHEILA SCHULLER COLEMAN

RUSSELL FALLS, TASMANIA, AUSTRALIA

A lesson from Winnie-the-Pooh

"Immediately Jesus reached out his hand and caught him."

MATTHEW 14:31

There's a Winnie-the-Pooh story in which Eeyore, the donkey, has fallen into a river. Pooh comes along, sees him there, and engages him in conversation.

Pooh asks, "Is the river cold?"

"Why, yes, as a matter of fact, it is," Eeyore replies.

Next, Pooh tells Eeyore that he really ought to be more careful. The donkey admits that that is true.

On further assessing the situation, Pooh has some rather bad news for his old friend. "I think you're sinking," he says.

And then, as Pooh prepares to go on his way, Eeyore humbly asks him, "If it's not too much trouble, would you mind rescuing me?"

Like Pooh, we all need to learn that when we see someone in trouble, the best thing to do is lend a helping hand. | ROBERT A. SCHULLER

GRAND TETON NATIONAL PARK, WYOMING, USA

Love expects the best

"Whatever is true, whatever is noble, whatever is right,
whatever is pure, whatever is lovely, whatever is admirable—
if anything is excellent or praiseworthy—think about such things."

PHILIPPIANS 4:8

Two kinds of birds fly over the California deserts—the hummingbird and the vulture. The vulture spends its time looking for rotten meat. Not so the hummingbird! It looks for the blooming cactus flowers hidden behind the rocks. Each bird finds what it's looking for.

Be a hummingbird, not a vulture. Build bridges, not walls. Believe the best about people and, oddly enough, they will become the people you expect them to be.

When Jesus was on earth he went to the "least" earth had to offer. He believed the best about them and let them know he believed they would become the "salt and light" of the world. And they did. This small band of fishermen became leaders of a great international movement of love and brotherhood.

Jesus asks us to do the same—believe the best about the worst!

| ROBERT H. SCHULLER

PHONE BOX, KIRKSTILE, LAKES DISTRICT, UK

Love that communicates

"...show mercy...do it cheerfully."

ROMANS 12:8

The opposite of love isn't hate—it's fear. Understanding this can open up communication with those who are hostile, mean, or vindictive.

I had to practice this when we were planning to construct a new building on the Crystal Cathedral garden grounds. Before going any further, we had to hold a public meeting with our community neighbors to obtain a building permit.

As people arrived, I sensed some strong negative vibrations from them. I greeted them congenially and silently prayed, "Lord, if you want to use me to bless these people tonight, I'm available."

That's when a miracle happened. God opened my eyes to understand that the people there were lonely, fearful, or hurting. My prayer continued, "God, let me, and our new building plans, minister hope and healing to those in need." God worked. There wasn't a single voice of opposition!

| ROBERT H. SCHULLER

ROTTNEST ISLAND, WESTERN AUSTRALIA, AUSTRALIA

In God's hands

"The righteous and the wise and what they do are in God's hands."

ECCLESIASTES 9:1

What does it mean to have God in your life? It means he's always with you. He watches over you when you sleep, and is there to greet you when you open your eyes in the morning. He is at the breakfast table when you're reading your morning newspaper or eating your bowl of Wheaties. He's there when you're lonely or when you have a house full of friends. He's there when the tears roll down your cheeks and when you're laughing hysterically.

You must constantly remind yourself that God is with you...wherever you are, whatever you're doing. No, he's not a cosmic snoop who's constantly looking over your shoulder to see what you're up to. He's there to comfort, support, and protect when you need him—and you *always* need him.

God is always with you. You're in his hands. | ROBERT A. SCHULLER

CLINGMAN'S DOME, GREAT SMOKY MOUNTAINS, TENNESSEE, USA

Rise above the opposition

*"Those who hope in the Lord will renew their strength.
They will soar on wings like eagles; they will run and not grow weary,
they will walk and not be faint."*

ISAIAH 40:31

Have you ever started a worthy and ambitious project with plenty of energy and an exciting vision, only to be waylaid by delays and opposition? That is the predicament the Jews found themselves in as they returned to Jerusalem from exile in Babylon to rebuild the temple so worship could resume.

The project started with flair and promise. But before long, mocking and opposition from those who wanted them to fail caused the workers to lose heart and turn their attention to their own projects. The project got stalled for over fifteen years. It wasn't until the people put God first in their hearts and actions again that the project resumed.

When discouragement and opposition overshadow your efforts, God will empower and lift your flagging spirit, strengthen your weary body, and lead you to success. | POWER FOR LIFE BIBLE

RAINBOW FALLS, NANTAHALA NATIONAL FOREST, NORTH CAROLINA, USA

Forego-it or go-for-it?

"Joshua and Caleb said, 'The land we passed through and explored is exceedingly good. The Lord...will lead us into that land, a land flowing with milk and honey, and he will give it to us.'"

NUMBERS 14:6-8

D o you see a glass of water as half full or half empty? Optimists see the glass as half full. A pessimist sees it as half empty. Same glass, different perspectives.

There's an old tale about two shoe salesmen who traveled to a primitive country to find new markets for their shoes. When they got off the ship, hundreds of barefoot natives greeted them. Nobody was wearing shoes. The salesmen headed straight for the local dispatch office. The first wired the president of his company: "I'm coming home. No shoes to be sold here. Nobody wears them." The second salesman sent an equally urgent message to his company's CEO: "Send thousands of shoes. *Nobody* wears them!"

It's a matter of perspective. The first salesman saw only the challenge. The second one saw great opportunity.

Choose optimism and turn your "forego-its" into "go-for-its!"

| ROBERT A. SCHULLER

GHOST GUM, PAPUNYA, NORTHERN TERRITORY, AUSTRALIA

Never give up

*"Persevere so that when you have done the will of God,
you will receive what he has promised."*

HEBREWS 10:36

I dreamed of being a physician. However, my studies suffered due to my over-involvement in extra-curricular activities. I sang in an opera, and accompanied vocalists—just to name a few. After an Organic Chemistry test I was sure I'd bombed, I called Dad in tears.

"Talk to your professor. See what he can do," he counseled.

Spirit sagging, I went to see my professor. My test was graded "D".

"I can't get into med school with a 'D' in chemistry," I told him. "And I can't let down the music department."

He offered, "Take an incomplete, then study hard over Christmas break. I'll give you a final when you get back."

Dad hired a tutor. I studied eighteen hours a day, aced the final, and discovered in the process that I love Organic Chemistry.

Never give up. God never gives up on you! | SHEILA SCHULLER COLEMAN

BRIDAL VEIL FALLS, YOSEMITE VALLEY, CALIFORNIA, USA

Push the button

*"He fell with his face to the ground and prayed, 'My Father, if it is possible,
may this cup be taken from me. Yet not as I will, but as you will.'"*

MATTHEW 26:39

The great Aswan High Dam on the Nile River is one of the largest ever constructed. It took eleven years to build and holds back 200 billion cubic yards of water. Twelve spinning turbines produce 12 billion kilowatts of power annually.

When construction of the dam was completed in 1972, Egyptian President Gamal Abdel Nasser had the privilege of pushing the button that started those huge turbines. Electricity began flowing through the lines, feeding power to Egypt, Sudan and surrounding territories.

Our lives are like that. When we, through a conscious act of the will, say, "God, I'm turning my life over to you. Do whatever you must to make me the person you want me to be"—that's when God releases his power in our lives.

Go ahead. Push the button. Let God take control of your life...every bit of it! | ROBERT A. SCHULLER

DAINTREE RAINFOREST, QUEENSLAND, AUSTRALIA

What's your power source?

"If you remain in me and I in you, you will bear much fruit;
apart from me you can do nothing."

JOHN 15:5

What source of power are you plugged in to? Appearance? Intelligence? Money? Career? There's nothing wrong, per se, with any of these. It's just the role you allow them to play in your life. If you rely on appearance to feel loveable, on intelligence to feel worthwhile, on money to get what you want, or on a successful career to feel important, you are missing out on the true source of living a fulfilled, rich, loving, satisfied life. You also run the risk of hurting others, losing valued relationships, and ending up with a pile of regrets at the end of your life. God wants better for you.

To experience true power in your life, plug in to God's Spirit. Plugging in to him will get you off reserve power and connected to the source of true power. | POWER FOR LIFE BIBLE

CRESTED BUTTE, COLORADO, USA

God's dreams are always so large
that they require his help to make them come true.

ROBERT H. SCHULLER

April

ELIOT FALLS, QUEENSLAND, AUSTRALIA

April fool's

"I said, 'I will confess my transgressions to the Lord.'
And you forgave the guilt of my sin."

PSALM 32:5

It was April Fool's Day and I was determined to fool Dad. Up early, I used a chair to reach the sugar bowl, emptied it, and filled it with salt thinking it would be undetectable.

I ran back to my room, got ready for school, then joined the family at the kitchen table for breakfast. Everyone poured a bowl of cereal. Dad added milk to his and lifted the sugar bowl. I almost burst waiting to yell, "April Fool's!"

Dad extended the bowl toward me and said, "Here, Sheila—you first."

Now what? I wasn't about to ruin my cereal. I had no choice but to 'fess up.

I learned then—father knows best! My Heavenly Father also knows best and can't be fooled. I recommend...always 'fess up before you mess up worse than you already have. | SHEILA SCHULLER COLEMAN

SUNSET OVER DOVE LAKE, TASMANIA, AUSTRALIA

Joy in the dark

"I have told you this so that my joy may be in you
and that your joy may be complete."

JOHN 15:11

One stormy day, the disciples were far out to sea when they were startled as a ghostly image appeared walking toward them on top of the waves. Out in the dark, Jesus called, "Do not be frightened. It is I!"

What does Jesus walking on water mean to us today? First, it means we can trust that he is the Son of God for he is the only person to have ever displayed power over atmospheric elements. Second, we can see how powerful Jesus really is, for if he has the power to walk on water, then surely he has the power to help us, no matter what our need.

Be encouraged to live your life with joy, trusting that Jesus is taking care of everything. For he is the Risen Savior, God's Son, the Creator, Omnipotent Lord over all—even the elements. | POWER FOR LIFE BIBLE

SUNSET, BREAKWATER LIGHTHOUSE, CAPE HENLOPEN STATE PARK, DELAWARE, USA

Surrender

"The mind of man plans his way, but the Lord directs his steps."

PROVERBS 16:9

Every year, thousands of people visit the San Juan Capistrano Mission in Southern California and try to catch the doves that flock to the ancient mission. They reach out with their hand, fingers open, and just as they are about to grasp the feet of the dove, it flaps its wings and flies away. So they try again...cautiously, slowly, furtively...but the bird escapes again.

The secret to catching a dove is this: You simply have to extend your hand, holding it out straight in front of you. Open your palm. Wait quietly. And the dove will come and rest in the middle of your hand.

Do you want God to guide you? Then surrender your soul, your mind, your spirit in the same way a dove surrenders to an open hand. If you do, God will take over your life and guide you. | ROBERT H. SCHULLER

GOD'S MARBLES, NORTHERN TERRITORY, AUSTRALIA

Hold fast to faith

"The testing of your faith produces perseverance."

JAMES 1:3

Faith is severely challenged when you don't see answers to prayer that you hoped for. After pouring your heart out, pleading with God to save a loved one or yourself only to have a miracle fail to appear, it is common to face a faith crisis.

Why did God not hear my prayers? Why didn't he give me the miracle I prayed for? Was my faith not strong enough? Did I not pray enough? Does God love me less than those he graces with the miraculous stories I've heard? Are others favored by God and I am not?

What do you have to lose by holding fast to faith? Nothing. What do you have to lose when you give in to despair? Everything! Choose to plant a seed of faith and believe that it will bloom. | SHEILA SCHULLER COLEMAN

RUSSELL FALLS, TASMANIA, AUSTRALIA

Amazing grace

"When Jesus saw their faith, he said to the paralyzed man,
'Son, your sins are forgiven.'"

MARK 2 : 1 - 5

Jesus said, "Which is easier? To forgive sins or to heal a paralytic?" He continued to say to the crowd, and then to the paralytic, "In order to show you that I have the authority to forgive sins, pick up your mat and go home." To everyone's amazement, the man stood up, picked up his mat, and walked out of the house!

How would you have answered the question—is it easier to forgive or to miraculously heal someone? In this miracle, Jesus makes it clear that even though he cares about our physical well-being and can perform miracles, it is even more important to him that our sins be forgiven. This was the first and foremost reason he came. This is still his number one priority for us—to forgive us.

Forgiveness—what a gift! Grace—how amazing! | POWER FOR LIFE BIBLE

OLD CAR, TASMANIA, AUSTRALIA

The price of forgiveness

*"If you hold anything against anyone, forgive them,
so that your Father in heaven may forgive you your sins."*

MARK 11:25

When I was a small boy, I remember getting my first and, perhaps, only spanking from my father for having hammered a nail into one of my parents' good chairs. After my father spanked me, I cried and said, "I'm sorry!"

Dad took me firmly by the arm and led me into the living room. He told me to pull the nail out of the chair and then said to me, "Look at the hole, Bob. You say you're sorry—and I believe you. I forgive you. But the hole is still there."

Forgiveness doesn't mean things can go back to the way they were. Forgiveness means you no longer have to carry with you the load of resentment and bitterness. You no longer wish the person who harmed you ill. Forgiveness is a choice. Today, choose to forgive! | ROBERT H. SCHULLER

EAST RANDOLPH, VERMONT, USA

White as snow

*"Though your sins are like scarlet, they shall be as white as snow;
though they are red as crimson, they shall be like wool."*

ISAIAH 1:18

You may look at your life and see the wrong things you've done. They may stand out like the scarlet "A" that Hester Prynne was forced to wear in Nathaniel Hawthorne's *Scarlet Letter*. But when God forgives he washes your sins so clean you can't even see them anymore.

It's like those laundry commercials where the homemaker is washing the dirtiest pile of laundry you've ever seen. The laundry is covered with grease stains, food stains, and you-name-it stains. She puts the whole pile into the washer, pours in the detergent, and a few seconds later—voila! She takes out the whitest, brightest, cleanest shirts, pants, and socks you've ever seen.

Don't be weighed down by guilt and regret. There is nothing you can do that is beyond the grace of God to forgive. | ROBERT A. SCHULLER

ON THE ROAD TO GUNDAGAI, NEW SOUTH WALES, AUSTRALIA

No other plan

*"How beautiful are the feet of those who bring good news,
who proclaim peace, who bring good tidings, and proclaim salvation."*

ISAIAH 52:7

I love to tell the story about a conversation that takes place in heaven. Jesus is talking to an angel who asks, "Jesus, you lived on earth and presented your message to the people there. But what happens now?"

Jesus answers, "Well, I trained my apostles and shared with them everything I know. They'll tell others, who will tell others...until the whole world has heard my message and knows my name."

"But, Jesus," the angel inquires, "what if they don't tell others?"

And Jesus replies, "I have no other plan."

Christ is counting on you and me to share the good news of Jesus Christ with the world—with our families, friends, neighbors, and everyone who needs to hear it. We are Christ's messengers and Christ's message to a spiritually lost and needy world. Who will you share his message with today?

| ROBERT A. SCHULLER

CHAPEL OF THE TRANSFIGURATION, GRAND TETON NATIONAL PARK, WYOMING, USA

Because of the cross

"But rejoice inasmuch as you participate in the sufferings of Christ, so that you may be overjoyed when his glory is revealed."

I PETER 4:13

The shocking fact about Christianity is the bold honesty with which followers of Jesus Christ recognize the reality of suffering.

The followers of Jesus were so inspired by his positive faith when he was nailed to a cross and died innocently in shame, that they launched a movement that put the cross on the towers of church steeples around the world.

The cross is the boldest, most beautiful "plus sign" in human history. This stunning symbol radiates hope and redemption. A shuddering minus has become a shining plus. At the foot of the cross, every hurt can be turned into a halo.

What the world needed two thousand plus years ago, it still needs today—a faith that avoids fantasy and confronts the raw reality of human anguish. A faith securely anchored at the foot of the cross. | ROBERT H. SCHULLER

FIELD OF RAINBOWS, SKAGIT VALLEY, WASHINGTON, USA

The indescribable gift

"If you...know how to give good gifts to your children, how much more will your Father in heaven give good gifts to those who ask him!"

MATTHEW 7:11

Though innocent, Jesus received a death sentence. A part of God's plan, it was done to provide a way for us to be redeemed and restored to fellowship with him even though we do not deserve it. We are not innocent, and we deserve a death sentence, but Jesus paid the price for us.

It is as if we were on trial, the jury comes in with a guilty verdict, the judge sentences us to death, and then a man walks into the courtroom and says, "Wait! I will die in this person's place. Let him (or her) go free." You are released and Jesus is taken away to die in your place.

What a gift! It is one that must not be taken lightly or without eternal gratitude. Praise God for his indescribable gift–his Son, Jesus Christ!

| POWER FOR LIFE BIBLE

MARBLEHEAD LIGHTHOUSE, LAKE ERIE, OHIO, USA

To the glory of God

"Let your light shine before others, that they may see your good deeds and glorify your Father in heaven."

MATTHEW 5:16

Martin Luther said, "If the world had treated me the way it treated God, I would have kicked the whole thing to pieces long ago." Other theologians have wrestled with this same question. Some say "God should have let the boat sink with Noah in it." Why does God bother with a race of people who treat him with arrogance, haughtiness, and pride?

The answer is simple. God created the human race and he loves mankind. So much so that he was willing to pay the price through the death of his Son to reconcile us to himself—to the glory of God. Only God can make the tough, tender; the arrogant, humble; the cynical, believing; and the insulting, polite. God's desire is to build a new culture within human society—a kingdom that will extend into eternity. | ROBERT H. SCHULLER

THE GARDEN TOMB, JERUSALEM

Victory over death

"Death has been swallowed up in victory."

1 CORINTHIANS 15:54

When Jesus cried, "It is finished!" the disciples thought the story was over. But God hadn't had the last word.

With a heavy heart and grieving spirit, Mary Magdalene went to the tomb early Easter morning. It was still dark. Mary was shocked to see the stone had been rolled away and that the tomb was empty. Thinking Jesus' body had been stolen, she sat weeping. Two angels asked why she was crying. Answering, she turned and saw a man she thought was the gardener. He spoke her name.

"Mary."

Mary knew it was Jesus. He was alive!

There are times you may think you've come to the end. You're discouraged, disappointed, and broken. But as you sit weeping, Jesus whispers your name and hope springs back to life.

God will have the last word—and it will be good.

POWER FOR LIFE BIBLE

SUNRISE OVER THE SEA OF GALILEE FROM MOUNT ARBEL, ISRAEL

Power over death

"For my Father's will is that everyone who looks to the Son and believes in him shall have eternal life, and I will raise them up at the last day."

JOHN 6:40

No fear surpasses the fear of death.

For most of us, all fears pale in comparison, even the fear of failure or shame. Death is so final, so irreversible. On the cross, Jesus proclaimed, "It is finished." Onlookers probably thought they would never see or speak to Jesus again. Jesus was saying by his outcry that the ultimate battle with Darkness was finished! The ransom was paid. Death was defeated once and for all.

The cross was not the end of the story; it was the beginning. The empty tomb shouts to us today that we are saved and have the promise and assurance of eternal life. Jesus died. He rose again. The empty tomb gives all who know him personally Christ's power over death. Christian—you have *nothing* to fear! | SHEILA SCHULLER COLEMAN

MARION LUTHERAN CHURCH, GUNDER, IOWA, USA

Life's most important decision

"For it is with your heart that you believe and are justified,
and it is with your mouth that you profess your faith and are saved."

ROMANS 10:10

It happened one Sunday morning, in the balcony of the First Reformed Church in Orange City, Iowa. Reverend Colenbrander closed his sermon by saying, "There is a young person here today who has never accepted Jesus Christ. That's where growth begins. Growth happens when you dare to do things you've never done before, when you trust an idea you never wanted to trust, and when you decide to be open to something you haven't been open to before."

He concluded with, "God sent Jesus Christ to be your Savior and Lord. Accept him this morning."

So up there in that old country church balcony, I bowed my head and said silently, "Yes, Jesus. I want to grow. I will follow you all my life. I'll trust you. Please be my Lord and best friend."

Today I invite you to do the same. | ROBERT H. SCHULLER

MITCHELL FALLS, WESTERN AUSTRALIA, AUSTRALIA

Give faithfully

"Give, and it will be given to you. A good measure, pressed down, shaken together and running over, will be poured into your lap. For with the measure you use, it will be measured to you."

LUKE 6:38

Everything we have belongs to God—the money in our pockets, the cars we drive, the houses we live in, the jobs we hold, the children we love, our health, our life, our very breath. We are simply managers of it.

We know God owns everything we have. But we struggle to affirm that in our hearts when there are car payments, house payments, medical bills, bikes, braces, broken arms, and an endless string of other family expenses that confront us every day.

Why give God a tenth of all we possess? Because it's his anyway!

When we tithe, we are investing in a future that pays a dividend that can never be lost. We are expressing thanksgiving to God for his goodness and provision. And we're accepting the honor of being called God's child.

Tithe faithfully, and God will bless you abundantly!

| ROBERT A. SCHULLER

OUTBACK OASIS, NORTHERN TERRITORY, AUSTRALIA

Hands above your own

"I know the Lord is always with me.
I will not be shaken, for he is right beside me."

PSALM 16:8

When my son Robert was nine years old he wanted to learn to drive my car. So one day I let him sit between my legs behind the steering wheel and drive the car around the ten-acre church grounds. His little white-knuckled hands strangled the steering wheel, but he managed to maneuver the turns and bring the car back to its parking spot. When we went home for lunch that day, you should have heard him boast to his mother and older sister, "I drove the car, Mommy, all by myself! Really I did!"

Happy but foolish child. My big hands were only a fraction of an inch over his all the time and my foot was on the gas pedal had I needed to take over.

The hand of Almighty God is never far away, so you can trust the future.

| ROBERT H. SCHULLER

HAY ROLLS, MICA, IDAHO, USA

Too little, too late

"For the Lord God is a sun and shield; the Lord bestows favor and honor; no good thing does he withhold from those whose walk is blameless."

PSALM 84:11

How many times have you sent an SOS to God but failed to get a response—or one that was too little, too late? When that happens, it feels as though our problems were not important enough, or our faith was too small. But it's not the importance of our problems, or his love for us, or the size of our faith that determines whether or not God responds to our cries for help. It is God's perfect plan that determines when and how he responds.

When the request is wrong, God says, "No." When the time is wrong, God says, "Slow." When we are not right, God says, "Grow." When everything is right, God says, "Go!"

Trust in God's perfect plan when his response feels like it's too little, too late. | SHEILA SCHULLER COLEMAN

DESERT OAKS, ULURU, NORTHERN TERRITORY, AUSTRALIA

Value that lasts

"And whatever you do, whether in word or deed,
do it all in the name of the Lord Jesus."

COLOSSIANS 3:17

A young boy's parents gave him a dollar and told him he could spend it any way he wanted. So, he went to the store. He passed by the candy...and the balloons. Then he headed for the toys and passed them by too, until he spotted a whistle...which he bought. The boy left the store blowing his new whistle. He blew it all the way home. But by the time he got home, he was already tired of his whistle. He threw the whistle on the ground and cried, "I spent all my money on this whistle and don't really want it after all."

Here was a boy who had a chance...and blew it! A silly story, but it makes a point: The "things" of this life aren't of much value. The only thing that lasts is what we do for Christ. | ROBERT H. SCHULLER

THE TWELVE APOSTLES, VICTORIA, AUSTRALIA

The secret of his strength

"He fell in love with a woman named Delilah…
who lured him into showing her the secret of his great strength."

JUDGES 16:4-5

Samson thought he had no limitations. He was the epitome of strength. Yet even Samson had his weakness. In his case, it was a beautiful woman who enticed him and tricked him into turning from his source of strength—GOD. It was only when Samson turned back to God that God restored his strength.

Your weaknesses, your disabilities, are defined by the degree to which you accept their limitations. If you see your weaknesses as limitations—be it fear, a lack of confidence, a lack of ability—then it will limit what you can do and be for God. But if you see your weaknesses as an opportunity for God's strength to be revealed, trusting him to help you overcome your fear, your lack of confidence, your inability—then his strength will be revealed through your weakness. | POWER FOR LIFE BIBLE

WHITSUNDAY ISLAND, QUEENSLAND, AUSTRALIA

Connect with a winner

"But thanks be to God, who always leads us in Christ's triumphal procession and uses us to spread the aroma of the knowledge of him everywhere."

2 CORINTHIANS 2:14

When my son Robert was a freshman in college he had a tough time with a course in Russian. "Dad," he told me, "I think I'm going to quit." He didn't. Perhaps I helped with that.

I was in New York and saw a huge poster of a football player sitting on the bench. He'd thrown down his helmet, mud was on his face, tears were rolling down his cheeks, and his elbows were on his knees. He looked dejected. The big words underneath the image read: *I quit.*

Then in a bottom corner of the poster, shown from far away, was a picture of a black hill, and on the hill was a cross. Underneath the cross were the words: *I didn't.*

I bought the poster and gave it to Robert.

Don't be a quitter. Connect with Christ and be a winner.

| ROBERT H. SCHULLER

LAKE TINAROO, QUEENSLAND, AUSTRALIA

A human being's worth

*"Christ died and returned to life
so that he might be the Lord of both the dead and the living."*

ROMANS 14:9

Ask a chemist what the value of a human being is and he'll tell you that you can reduce the average body of bones, flesh, hair, and blood to a handful of chemicals that can be purchased for just a few dollars at a chemical store. You're not worth much according to a chemist.

The cynic will tell you, "Stick your finger in a bowl of water, pull it out and see how big a hole is left, then you'll know how important you are."

So, what *is* a human being worth? That depends. Disconnected, on his own, a human being is a big waste. But take that life and connect it to Jesus Christ, let him redeem it, and then what do you think it is worth? It's priceless! God makes it so. | ROBERT H. SCHULLER

AMISH FARM, LANCASTER, PENNSYLVANIA, USA

Created to connect

"Be devoted to one another in love.
Honor one another above yourselves."

ROMANS 12:10

We all need family and friendships. The most recent neurobiological studies reveal that we humans are hardwired for connections to other people as well as to spiritual meaning and purpose. This means God created us to be in fellowship with others as well as fellowship with him and his purpose for our lives. If God created us to have meaningful connections with others, primarily through families and friendships, God will not leave us lonely.

If we are lonely, we need to ask ourselves: "Am I lonely because I have withdrawn and isolated myself from the people who are most important in my life?"

God did not create you to be alone. If you long to have love in your life, ask God to provide it. Then take the step of faith and discover the love you long for. | POWER FOR LIFE BIBLE

MURRAY RIVER JETTY, SOUTH AUSTRALIA, AUSTRALIA

Disconnected by distractions?

"Be still before the Lord and wait patiently for him."

PSALM 37:7

Mother Teresa maintained that distractions are the single most interfering disconnection between God and you. Can you think of something that distracted you from spending time with God? Of course! All of us can! There's nothing more frustrating than sitting down with your Bible, beginning to read or pray only to be broadsided by a passel of distractions.

That's why some people write their prayers in a prayer journal. The act of writing your prayers helps you stay focused. If you are easily distracted, keep a pad of paper and a pencil handy so when things you need to do pop into your mind, you can write them down to tackle later and resume your time with God. Tackle the distractions so you can clear the path to connect with God. It's worth it! | SHEILA SCHULLER COLEMAN

FRASER ISLAND, QUEENSLAND, AUSTRALIA

The loneliness of failing

"Apart from me you can do nothing."

JOHN 15:5

Loneliness touches all of our lives at different times and in different ways. I remember a time when I was facing a horrendous failure and felt like I was sinking. What I learned is that when faced with failure and you don't want to admit it, the first step back is saying: "I need help!"

In my book *The Be-Happy Attitudes*, I began with the beatitude, "Blessed are the poor in spirit." Being poor in spirit means you are able to step out of your denial and admit to yourself and others, "I need help—I can't do it alone!" Only then will joy and peace of mind return.

Cure the loneliness of failing—learn to join the human race. Admit your vulnerability. Own up to the fact that you, too, fail. Then step outside your comfort zone and ask for help. | ROBERT H. SCHULLER

KINGS CANYON, NORTHERN TERRITORY, AUSTRALIA

Fear less

"When I am afraid, I put my trust in you."

PSALM 56:3

One day as Donna and I were walking down the streets of La Paz, a little village on the Sea of Cortez in Mexico, we came across a shop specializing in scuba-diving excursions.

We talked to the proprietor who enthusiastically told us about El Bajo, an underwater mountain ten miles off the coast, the top of which comes within forty-five feet of the surface. He explained that schools of fish congregate there, but the main reason people like to dive there is for the hammerhead sharks.

I was sold. But selling Donna on the idea was quite another matter. Finally, she agreed to go. The dive turned out to be everything and more than the man had promised.

I wonder how often we miss beautiful "God opportunities" because of fear. Next time fear knocks at your door—let faith open it. | ROBERT A. SCHULLER

BALI HAI, KAUAI, HAWAII, USA

Are you down? Look up!

"I lift up my eyes to the mountains—where does my help come from?
My help comes from the Lord, the Maker of heaven and earth."

PSALM 121:1-2

Where can we go when we need help? The psalmist tells us we find help when we lift our eyes to the hills. He continues, "My help comes from the Lord who made heaven and earth."

Wow! When we are spiritually struggling, an emergency call to the God of the universe brings him to our rescue! He is just one prayer away. His power saves. His power can invigorate your faith. He loves and longs to help his children. He is *never* too busy and your problems are never too insignificant—he knows you need him. It's up to you to make the call. It's up to you to look to him for help.

When things look down—look up—to the hills—where your help comes from! Your help comes from the Lord, who made heaven and earth!

SHEILA SCHULLER COLEMAN

TWILIGHT PALMS, LANGKAWI, MALAYSIA

The multiplicative principle

"Taking the five loaves and the two fish and looking up to heaven, Jesus gave thanks and broke them...They all ate and were satisfied."

LUKE 9:16-17

Have you ever felt your efforts were too meager to make a difference? Or that you were inadequate compared to others in terms of your financial resources, intellect, talent, or appearance? Have you ever thought *If only I had more...[you fill in the blank], I could make a real difference?*

Many of us feel as though our meager gifts, our inadequate efforts, are insufficient for God. Yet all God asks for are "five loaves and two fishes" (Luke 9:10-17). Nothing is too small when Jesus uses it. Nothing is meager or inadequate when Jesus blesses it. Nobody is insignificant when Jesus chooses him or her.

Where do you need God to take something small in your life and multiply it to provide not only what you need, but more than enough?

| POWER FOR LIFE BIBLE

BARRENJOEY LIGHTHOUSE, NEW SOUTH WALES, AUSTRALIA

Plug in to the light

"The light shines in the darkness,
and the darkness has not overcome it."

JOHN 1:5

Take a suitcase filled with darkness into a room filled with light. When you open it, will the darkness from the suitcase spill out and dispel the light of the room, engulfing it in pitch darkness? Of course not! Just the opposite will occur. The light of the room will instantly flood the suitcase with light.

Having completed such an experiment, what conclusion would you draw? Which is more powerful, the light or the darkness?

Ah, of course. Light is far more powerful than darkness! Then why do you fear the darkness? As a Christian, you have the power of the eternal light source available to you. No matter how dark your life may become, all you have to do is remember to tap into the light. You can trust that the light will always outshine the darkness! | SHEILA SCHULLER COLEMAN

LINCOLN BOYHOOD NATIONAL MEMORIAL, LINCOLN CITY, INDIANA

When someone believes in you

"When the angel of the Lord appeared to Gideon,
he said, 'The Lord is with you, mighty warrior.'"

JUDGES 6:12

Edna May Buchanan made international news when she received the Pulitzer Prize in Journalism in 1986. But what you may not know is that Edna May was born into poverty. She wore hand-me-down clothes. Her home life was poor at best. And her self-image suffered countless blows.

One day she was asked to write a paper for school. As the teacher was handing back the papers, she gave Edna May's paper to her and commented, "Edna May, when you write your first book, dedicate it to me!"

That comment, made by a respected teacher to a young girl in shabby clothes, sitting behind a desk in the seventh grade, changed her life. Why? Because Edna May believed it! From that moment forward, Edna May Buchanan's destiny was shaped. Her self-image was forever changed because somebody believed in her. | ROBERT H. SCHULLER

PILE VALLEY, FRASER ISLAND, QUEENSLAND, AUSTRALIA

Doors of opportunity

"Rejoice with those who rejoice;
mourn with those who mourn."

ROMANS 12:15

I was the first church volunteer when we moved from Chicago to begin a new church. With no income for help, Dad's office was a bedroom at home. When the doorbell rang, Mom—always busy with home and infant—would ask, "Get it, will you, Sheila?"

At four I knew when the caller had been crying or was nervous as I'd walk them to Dad's "office."

Even after the church could support an office and secretary, people still came to our house at all hours. I overheard it all—a mother whose son drowned, a father whose son accidentally shot his sister, the teenager who lost a foot in a motorcycle accident.

There are always hurting people. An open door can transform the lives of those who open the door *and* those who walk through if they rely on God's Spirit. | SHEILA SCHULLER COLEMAN

GLORY OF SPRING, TASMANIA, AUSTRALIA

God's love blooms
when we love each other.

ROBERT H. SCHULLER

May

COLES BAY, TASMANIA, AUSTRALIA

Letting go, finding gain

"Whoever finds their life will lose it,
and whoever loses their life for my sake will find it."

MATTHEW 10:39

E aster being one of Dad and Robert's busiest days of the year, we Schullers celebrate it with a brunch the day before. With nineteen children, the Easter egg hunt is always anticipated eagerly.

When a preschooler our son, Christopher toddled through the room with Mom's prized teapot dangling from his arm. Dad ran to rescue it.

"Stuck," mumbled Chris. Dad saw that inside the narrow opening, Chris's hand was in a tight fist.

"Open your hand, Chris," Dad instructed.

"No. Egg," he retorted.

"Let go of the egg, Chris."

Dad took a larger egg from the mantel, offered it to Chris, and as Chris let go of the egg he'd been clinging to, Dad caught the teapot in his free hand.

How often has God had a bigger blessing in store for you but you miss it because you are unwilling to let go of the small blessing? Gain comes from letting go and trusting God! | SHEILA SCHULLER COLEMAN

RAINBOW, VICTORIA FALLS, ZIMBABWE

Breath of life

"The Lord God formed a man from the dust of the ground and breathed into his nostrils the breath of life, and the man became a living being."

GENESIS 2:7

ife begins with a single breath and then that very breath sustains you. How fragile and yet how strong is a single breath. You can't see it. You can't capture it. You can't store it up. Yet, the life that is inherent in each breath is enough to infuse life and power into you. God is your Breath of Life.

He breathed his life into you. Your Creator's breath of life is what empowers you to live an abundant life. Breathe in faith, exhale doubt. Breathe in hope, exhale despair. Breathe in peace, exhale anxious thoughts. Breathe in the power of the Holy Spirit and feel the love, the mercy, and the power of God at work within you! | SHEILA SCHULLER COLEMAN

SUNRISE, WAMBERAL BEACH, NSW, AUSTRALIA

Born again

"For you have been born again…
through the living and enduring word of God."

1 PETER 1:23

In the early one-room schoolhouses, students had their own slates on which they did their work. The teacher would frequently ask them to hold up their slates to see how they were doing. Slates are easily wiped clean. So the metaphor of a *clean slate* inspires a feeling of hope and being reborn.

Although it is impossible to live life without making a mistake, we can wipe the slate clean and start over. This is what Jesus was telling Nicodemus when he said, "I tell you, no one can see the kingdom of God without being born again" (John 3:5).

Have you been born again? If you have, then it's up to you to tell others about how they can have the assurance of eternal life. If you have not been born again, there's no time like the present. | POWER FOR LIFE BIBLE

MITCHELL FALLS, WESTERN AUSTRALIA, AUSTRALIA

Washed clean

*"Wash away all my iniquity
and cleanse me from my sin."*

PSALM 51:2

One morning I headed for the coffee pot to pour a cup of coffee. Looking down I noticed that there was about half-an-inch of black, yucky stuff in the bottom of the cup. It's what is left over when I don't wash the cup out and it sits on my desk for a few days.

The outside of the cup looked great, but the inside was a gooey mess. Once I washed it out, the cup was clean enough to drink anything. In fact, it was so clean I decided to have a nice, clean cup of water!

When Christ comes into your life, he cleans you up inside the same way I cleaned the inside of that cup. He scrubs away all the guilt and shame, the failures and fears, and all your sins—and he washes you clean!

ROBERT A. SCHULLER

COUNTRY GARDEN, VICTORIA, AUSTRALIA

A seed of faith

"I do believe; help me overcome my unbelief!"

MARK 9:24

Too little faith? Then you're in good company. Mary, the sister of Lazarus, suffered from too little faith. Peter denied Christ three times. If that's not too little faith, then what is?

Yet, too little faith is just enough faith! It only takes a tiny seed of faith to keep your faith alive. If you lack even that, simply ask for faith or even for some more faith. Ask God to plant a seed of faith in your heart today. Ask him to take that too-little seed and to germinate it and allow it to grow into a large bush, bearing even more seeds.

Only God can *plant* a seed of faith. Only God can *grow* a seed of faith. Only God can *count* the seeds in one little faith seed. He is waiting for one thing—you to ask for it! | SHEILA SCHULLER COLEMAN

RAGGED POINT, BIG SUR COAST, CALIFORNIA, USA

God sees the big picture

"The eyes of the Lord your God are continually on it,
from the beginning of the year to its end."

DEUTERONOMY 11:12

Most of us are short-sighted. We see only the temporary struggles, aggravations, and disappointments. God, on the other hand, is very long-sighted. He sees all of eternity. When God looks at your life, it's like he's picking up a roll of film, stretching it out, and seeing everything at the same time.

God sees every action within the context of the whole. He knows what the results of each step or misstep you take will be, and how he is going to work things out so that the big picture comes together as a blessing. Nothing falls below God's radar. He sees it all. And on occasion he gives you just a sneak peak of his bigger picture.

What do you do in the interim? All you can do is trust—believe that God has your best interest at heart. | ROBERT A. SCHULLER

SEQUOIA FOREST, CALIFORNIA, USA

Rooted in God's garden

"It was majestic in beauty...for its roots went down to abundant waters."

EZEKIEL 31:7

Just try to get bamboo out of a garden once it has taken root in your soil. Or try to rid your lawn of crab grass once those seeds have found your yard. The roots of these plants are tenacious! They burrow deep and hold on tight!

What if your spiritual life were as deeply rooted in your faith? Then when the storms of life battered you, your roots would keep you anchored. When the rains of disappointment threatened to drown you, your roots would keep you from being washed away. When temptations threatened to pull you down and discard you like weeds, your roots would survive to sprout again.

Send your roots deep into God's garden. Spend time in prayer, in fellowship with other Christians, and in reading God's word. Then when the storms of life come, you'll stay firmly rooted! | SHEILA SCHULLER COLEMAN

LIGHTNING, SOUTH AUSTRALIA, AUSTRALIA

God's thunderous voice

"He gathers the lambs in his arms and carries them close to his heart."

ISAIAH 40:11

Iowa's summer thunderstorms are magnificent. Skies light up, rumbles crackle.

Once, Dad carried me onto the porch. Holding me tightly, he said, "Sheila, look how magnificent this is! You're catching a glimpse of God's power. Instead of fearing it, regard it as God's voice."

That might scare most children, but I was taught never to fear God. In Dad's arms I was thrilled watching majestic flashes, hearing the rumble of thunder.

God's thunderous voice gave me great comfort as a child. Of course, thunder isn't really his voice, but it does remind me that his power is there to help carry me. His strong, loving arms are there to hold me, just like my dad's were when I was a child. God's thunderous voice assures me that I am not alone during tough times. The God of the Universe holds me and protects me. | SHEILA SCHULLER COLEMAN

LONE CYPRESS, CARMEL, CALIFORNIA, USA

God is my strength

"The Lord is my strength and my defense;
he has become my salvation."

EXODUS 15:2

Some people who appear weak and feeble actually reveal God's strength. Though unable to see, hear, or speak, Helen Keller taught us by her life what it means to see without eyes, understand without ears, and communicated with limited speech.

All of us have weaknesses, shortcomings, limitations. Maybe yours is a physical infirmity or an intellectual limitation, such as a learning disability. Maybe you have an emotional weakness or even a mental health issue such as Alzheimer's or a bipolar disorder. Or, maybe you're challenged by something as simple as a weakness in math.

Regardless of the degree of severity of your weakness, God is stronger than your weakness. The more severe your weakness, the more God's strength will be revealed.

God is merciful and faithful. He will help you face your weaknesses head-on and overcome them with his strength! | POWER FOR LIFE BIBLE

SHARK BAY, WESTERN AUSTRALIA, AUSTRALIA

Perfect peace

"You will keep in perfect peace those whose minds are steadfast,
because they trust in you."

ISAIAH 26:3

A friend who often traveled the Atlantic told me this story: "One time our ship was caught in a terrible Atlantic storm. It seemed as if the ship would be ripped apart and split at the seams. The storm went on for days. Finally one night it reached its peak and mob panic was about to break out. At that moment the captain began recounting the ship's history: 'This ship has gone through many storms—some worse than this.' After he finished describing the storms the ship had survived, the captain said in a strong, confident voice, 'So! We will trust this good ship and God who rides the storm, and we will see it through!' And with that, everyone felt at peace."

Prayer is the ship that takes us through life's storms. Board that ship and God will see you through. | ROBERT H. SCHULLER

WAMBERAL BEACH, NEW SOUTH WALES, AUSTRALIA

Awaken my soul

"Awake, my soul! Awake, harp and lyre! Awaken the dawn."

PSALM 57:8

Sleep brings restoration. But there comes a time to wake up and use your renewed power to make a positive difference. Similarly, your soul may be in sleep mode from time to time. God allows these times to refresh you. When your faith awakens, it is that much stronger, that much more powerful.

If your faith is in sleep mode, immerse yourself in God's word. Study a psalm a day, find positive Christian community. PRAY. Ask God to awaken your soul and your faith.

If all else fails, find someone who needs you. ENGAGE in helping that person. Nothing awakens you more than throwing yourself into a situation where your faith must be used.

So, awaken my soul, O Lord. Stream into my life with the sunlight that renews and refreshes my faith! Amen. | SHEILA SCHULLER COLEMAN

FIRST LIGHT, TERRIGAL BEACH, NEW SOUTH WALES, AUSTRALIA

Morning has broken

"In the morning, Lord, you hear my voice;
in the morning I lay my requests before you and wait expectantly."

PSALM 5:3

The sun has risen. The Son has risen. Night is over, the gloom dispelled by the first rays of a bright new day. Hope is reborn. Even though our previous attempts failed, the past brought tears and disappointments, and night always comes again—we have a choice. We can choose to focus on the morning or the night, the light or the darkness, our successes or our failures. And the truth is: Every day includes a blessing.

Believe in the morning. Believe in the God of miracles. Believe in the God of love. Believe in the God who is more powerful than any disappointment, any night, any end of day. As sure as there is life on earth, morning always comes again. Indeed...morning is breaking right now... somewhere! | SHEILA SCHULLER COLEMAN

LAKE COONGIE, SOUTH AUSTRALIA, AUSTRALIA

Breaking into song

"The season of singing has come, the cooing of doves is heard in our land."

SONG OF SOLOMON 2:12

There is no more beautiful time of day than when the birds are singing in the early morning. The darkness of night gives way to dawn as it breaks forth in regal splendor, its golden arms outstretched across the sky to bathe the earth in joy and hope.

The time of the singing of the birds reminds us that we've been given another chance; that new opportunities are born with each new sunrise. It's a chance to start life over once more, to dream new dreams, to set new goals. A brilliant idea comes into your mind and just as the concept is conceived, the birds begin singing again, springing the world into action with their melodic song, offering hope and joy.

Listen—can you hear the birds sing? | ROBERT H. SCHULLER

WAHCLELLA FALLS, COLUMBIA WILDERNESS, OREGON, USA

Lesson from the ant

"Look at the ant...consider its ways and be wise!"

PROVERBS 6:6

One morning I was sitting in the backyard preparing my Sunday morning message when I noticed a platoon of ants moving in formation along the sidewalk. As my eyes followed them, I noticed the one bringing up the rear. He was several paces behind and struggling along with a straw in his mouth. The straw looked to be ten times his length and several times his weight. I watched, fascinated, as the ant approached a crevice in the sidewalk. *He'll fall into the crack and the straw will pin him in place,* I thought.

Never underestimate the capabilities of an ant! The ant took his unwieldy straw, laid it over the crevice, and walked across it to the other side. Then he picked it up and kept going.

That ant taught me a lesson: Burdens can be used as a bridge to a miracle.

| ROBERT A. SCHULLER

DIMOND GORGE, WESTERN AUSTRALIA, AUSTRALIA

Refreshing streams

"Times of refreshing...come from the Lord."

ACTS 3:19

Climbing a dry, rocky, barren hill, you put one foot in front of the other. It is sheer will power that carries you along determined to reach a high place. Turning around, you look behind you at the dusty lowlands below and see a stream—meandering like a rippling breeze—with lush verdant trees lining its banks. Hope springs within as you realize you've been saved.

Spiritual refreshment finds its way into your life when you least expect it. Thank God for powerfully providing lifesaving streams when you need them most! Suddenly you feel the refreshing movement of the Holy Spirit as he sweeps through you and rains his presence in your life. Hallelujah!

| SHEILA SCHULLER COLEMAN

OUTBACK ROAD, NORTHERN TERRITORY, AUSTRALIA

Processionary caterpillars

"Do you have eyes but fail to see, and ears but fail to hear?"

MARK 8:18

Jean Henri Fabre, a famous French naturalist, spent years experimenting with processionary caterpillars. The caterpillars attach themselves to one another and, with eyes at half-mast, move along as a unit in a blind-leading-the-blind fashion.

Fabre once arranged a line of the caterpillars in a rotating ring by attaching the first caterpillar to the last so the procession had no beginning or end. He put the ring on top of a large flowerpot and watched the woolly creatures plod around and around.

Seven days passed. Finally, overtaken by exhaustion and starvation, the ring of caterpillars died together. Any one of them could have stopped at any time and rested and eaten. But they didn't.

How often are you like those caterpillars? You don't look for a better way or dare to divert from the beaten path to take a new direction.

ROBERT A. SCHULLER

CAPE LEVEQUE, WESTERN AUSTRALIA, AUSTRALIA

Take one step

"By faith Abraham, when called to go to a place he would later receive
as his inheritance, obeyed and went, even though
he did not know where he was going."

HEBREWS 11:8

Abraham had it "made in the shade" when God asked him to leave it all behind. God gave Abraham an impossible dream. "You will be the father of a great nation," he said. And God promised Abraham this nation, Israel, would be blessed and would be a blessing to other nations.

It's easy to follow God when he asks us to do something we're familiar with. But when he calls us to step into uncharted territory where we feel inadequate or unprepared, that takes extreme faith. Abraham bravely stepped out in faith, and in that act of obedience became the model of extreme faith.

What is God calling you to do? All he asks is that you take one step for now. Don't let the comfort and security of your present position keep you from experiencing all God has for you. Step out in faith today!

| POWER FOR LIFE BIBLE

WOMBAT TARN, TASMANIA, AUSTRALIA

Diamonds in the rough

"I have refined you, though not as silver;
I have tested you in the furnace of affliction."

ISAIAH 48:10

Having majored in Chemistry, I found the diamond factory in Amsterdam fascinating. My husband, Jim, our sons and I were back for the first time since Dad's accident caused cerebral hemorrhaging requiring two emergency brain surgeries. Whereas we all were fascinated by the expertise of the cutters and dazzling stones, I was amazed at how diamonds are formed.

They are nothing but carbon—the same kind you find in lead pencils!

What makes them so different? Heat and pressure. Carbon under intense heat and pressure forms a lattice-like structure assuming different properties.

Without heat and pressure you are soft as pencil lead. When subjected to intense heat and pressure, you are strengthened, refined, and polished. God doesn't cause the fires of life, but he does use them to refine you into a spiritual gem reflecting his love and power to everyone you meet.

| SHEILA SCHULLER COLEMAN

BIG DADDY SAND DUNE, SOSSUSVLEI, NAMIBIA

Whose voice do you listen to?

"Encourage one another and build each other up,
just as in fact you are doing."

1 THESSALONIANS 5:11

We've all known persons who are talented, skilled, and full of potential. And yet, when you try to inspire or encourage them you can feel their resistance. They don't listen to you. They don't believe you. There's another voice they're listening to—a voice inside them that's saying, "He's putting you on. You can't trust him." It's a voice that tells them, "Don't try. Don't take that risk—you'll just get hurt." It's a voice that says, "Who do you think you are? You don't have the looks, the money, the intellect, the connections, or the talent."

One human being. Two distinctly different voices. They're whispering to you. At times, they're shouting! So, which voice are you going to listen to? Here's my advice: Believe in the people who believe in you!

| ROBERT H. SCHULLER

MORRO BAY, CALIFORNIA, USA

Leaving safe harbors

"He replied, 'You of little faith, why are you so afraid?' Then he got up and rebuked the winds and the waves, and it was completely calm."

MATTHEW 8:26

I love being on the ocean...feeling the waves rock me, and the ocean breeze and salt water on my face. It's an invigorating experience!

But I see boats in the harbor that never leave their moorings. How can I tell? By the barnacles covering the bottoms of the boats. Boats that just sit in the harbor never have to worry about storms or encounter rough waters.

But boats aren't made to stay in the harbor; they're made to sail the seas... to face storms and waves. And so are you!

You were made for a purpose and finding that purpose means going through some storms and challenges along the way.

Are you stuck in safe harbors? Unfurl the sails. Venture out to deep waters. God will go with you. There's nothing to fear.

| ROBERT A. SCHULLER

DELICATE ARCH, ARCHES NATIONAL PARK, UTAH, USA

Hurts into halos

"Blessed are those who persevere under trial,
because when they have stood the test, they will receive the crown of life
that God has promised to those who love him."

JAMES 1:12

Abandonment is one hurt I have never experienced. But my best friend did—his name is Jesus.

He was born a Jew, brought up in a good family, and lived the faith. His life was unstained by selfishness or sin. He experienced the hurt of rejection, grief, humiliation, injustice, and was left to slowly bleed to death on a shameful cross between two criminals. He experienced hell's torment when his Father abandoned him: "My God, My God, why have you forsaken me?" But the God he loved and served so obediently never answered his painful question.

Why? It's the question we all long to know the answer to. It's the one question God is not obligated to answer.

Faith grows through trusting God. When you can't find the answers, move ahead with quiet trust and God will turn your hurts into halos.

| ROBERT H. SCHULLER

AMERICAN BASIN, COLORADO, USA

Gains or losses?

*"But whatever were gains to me
I now consider loss for the sake of Christ."*

PHILIPPIANS 3:7

I s loss always negative? Are valleys always to be avoided? Is loss of a job always the end of something good?

The normal response to loss is grief, avoidance, even anger. But loss can be a good thing. Sometimes loss forces you to make a life-saving change. Losing a job can propel you to learn a new skill that leads you to a productive new career. Failure to get into a particular school might direct you to the school where God wants you to meet someone special. Loss of revenue can motivate you to examine your budget to learn where there have been extravagances. Spending time in the valleys can challenge you to look to the hills and keep your eyes on Christ.

When loss forces you to focus on Christ—it is ALWAYS a gain!

| SHEILA SCHULLER COLEMAN

MOSSMAN GORGE, QUEENSLAND, AUSTRALIA

Finding inner strength

"I pray that out of his glorious riches he may strengthen you with power through his Spirit in your inner being."

EPHESIANS 3:16

I recall a missionary in India telling how he was kneeling by his bed praying one night when a giant python uncoiled itself from the rafters and wrapped itself around his body. These words of Scripture flashed into his mind, "In quietness and confidence shall be your strength." The missionary said he received strength from God to remain so calm and so brave that he never moved. He just kept meditating.

Had he struggled, had he hesitated, had he tensed up, the coils would have been constricted and the missionary would have been crushed. Instead, he prayed. He waited. He became calm, remained poised, and didn't move. After several very long minutes, the snake uncoiled itself and slithered out the door.

God will give you the courage you need when you need it. Dare to trust him for it. | ROBERT H. SCHULLER

PICCANINNY CREEK, WESTERN AUSTRALIA, AUSTRALIA

Communication connection

*"My dear brothers and sisters, take note of this:
Everyone should be quick to listen and slow to speak."*

JAMES 1:19

Relationships depend on open communication. And effective communication leads to connection.

Unfortunately, our culture has lost its manners in conversation. People talk over each other or often talk at the same time. Society suffers from a communication breakdown—a cultural meltdown in what used to be common dignity in dialogue.

Dialogue is meant to be an exchange of ideas; one person speaking while others listen, back and forth. Talk shows that began as insightful dialogues have disintegrated into free-for-alls. This rudeness marks a cultural decline that threatens courteous communication as we lose the art of polite listening.

Communication is a God-given tool to be used to establish and enjoy relationships. We must learn sensible ways to communicate that don't overstress us and that strengthen our relationships.

Cultivate your conversation manners and you'll reap the rewards of meaningful human connection. | ROBERT H. SCHULLER

STATUE OF LIBERTY, NEW YORK, USA

Let freedom ring

"If the Son sets you free, you will be free indeed."

JOHN 8:36

The United States of America was based and built on freedom—something we hold dear as a democracy. People throughout the centuries have fought long and hard to achieve that freedom. Yet there are times when our exercise of freedom undermines the very things many fought so hard to obtain.

Freedom comes with a price. Many have paid the ultimate price for freedom with their lives in service to our country. Their service offers us an opportunity to worship freely, hear God's word taught openly, live in peace, and pursue life, liberty, and happiness.

Today, let's also remember the price Christ paid on the cross for us, thereby setting us free us from the tyranny of sin in our lives. True freedom comes from personal sacrifice, personal surrender, and personal service. So let freedom ring! | ROBERT A. SCHULLER

PIPELINE BEACH, OAHU, HAWAII, USA

Believe the best

"Love is patient, love is kind."

1 CORINTHIANS 13:4

I recall an article that appeared in *Psychology Today* reporting the results of a study they did on trust. Researchers investigated how trust affects human development and character. And believe it or not, the researchers concluded that trusting people are rarely taken advantage of.

I'm guessing the reason trusting people are seldom deceived may be related to this psychological truth: *I am not what I think I am; I am not what you think I am; I am what I think you think I am.*

People tend to become the person they think you imagine them to be. It's a form of self-fulfilling prophecy. So if you believe the best about a bad person and keep believing it, more often than not, that person will become the good person you believed them to be. It's tough to do, but it really works!

ROBERT H. SCHULLER

HAASTS BLUFF, NORTHERN TERRITORY, AUSTRALIA

God's honor

"And if I go and prepare a place for you,
I will come back and take you to be with me that you also may be where I am."

JOHN 14:3

The story is told of a little Scottish lassie who lay dying. Her pastor came to her and asked, "Lassie, if you die, are you sure you'll go to heaven?"

"Oh yes," she answered.

"How can you be sure?" the pastor persisted.

"Well," she replied, "Jesus promised, 'anyone who comes to me I will in no wise cast out.' I came to Jesus and accepted his love. He would never throw me away."

"But what if God forgets his promise?" the pastor inquired.

"Then he would lose more than I would," the girl replied. "I would only lose my soul. He would lose his honor."

The core of God's character is honor. He has promised you the spirit of Christ so you can treat your fellow others with great dignity. Remember how much he loves you. He will not turn you away. | ROBERT H. SCHULLER

KALUMBURU ROAD, KIMBERLEY, WESTERN AUSTRALIA, AUSTRALIA

Pay the toll

"Rejoice always, pray continually, give thanks in all circumstances;
for this is God's will for you in Christ Jesus."

1 THESSALONIANS 5:16-18

You're on an adventure. A pilgrimage. A trip and a tour through a land where you've never traveled before. Some decision you made somewhere, sometime, put you on this path, and you're now surprised at the toll gate. You chose the path, not knowing the price.

Warning! Don't make the impertinent, unintelligent, and cynical assumption that the price is too high.

Yes, the price you have to pay might seem high, but recall all of the pleasures, satisfactions, and benefits you received along the way and your heart will move from pain to praise.

Pay the toll and thank God for the trip you've had!

ROBERT H. SCHULLER

THE TWELVE APOSTLES, VICTORIA, AUSTRALIA

Challenging daily contradictions

"Blessed are those who persevere under trial."

JAMES 1:12

Daily living is full of challenging contradictions. But learning to deal positively with these contradictions can unleash creative possibilities.

I'll never forget the story of the janitor who was sulking because he had a big mess to clean up. That mess ultimately proved to be the best thing that ever happened to him.

Murray Spangler desperately needed his janitor job, but he hated scooping up all the tiny dust particles he encountered doing his work. One day an idea came to him: *What would happen if I used suction?* If he could suck up all those tiny particles, maybe this job would be much easier.

What was the outcome of confronting his daily challenge? Murray Spangler invented the Hoover vacuum cleaner. By confronting his daily contradiction with possibility thinking, he transformed his greatest annoyance into his greatest success. So can you. | ROBERT H. SCHULLER

LIFFEY FALLS, TASMANIA, AUSTRALIA

Time to recharge!

"Be filled with the Spirit...sing from your heart to the Lord."

EPHESIANS 5:18-19

Have you ever recharged a battery that held a charge at first, then over time became less and less able to be recharged until finally, you needed a power cord or a new battery altogether? The same principle holds true for your spiritual batteries.

You are powerless by yourself. You are not the Energizer Bunny®. You can plug into friends or family members, hoping they can jump-start you or be your source of energy. Even though God *can* use others, when you fail to recharge at the true power source—Jesus Christ, your Creator, God Almighty—you cannot expect your batteries to be fully recharged. You cannot expect *any* other charge to hold for long.

Recharge at the true source—God, his Holy Spirit, the word of God—especially in the psalms! You can trust your batteries are truly recharged.

| SHEILA SCHULLER COLEMAN

MILLAA MILLAA FALLS, QUEENSLAND, AUSTRALIA

Your personal mission statement

*"Do not neglect your gift, which was given you...
when the body of elders laid their hands on you."*

1 TIMOTHY 4:14

The human spirit has an inextinguishable hunger for a cause so consuming that it can fill the emptiness of the soul with pride, purpose, and pleasure. To turn your dreams into goals, you must write a positive personal mission statement.

A mission statement will keep you focused on the purpose of your life and keep you on course through the evolving challenges and achievements of it.

How do you find your life's high and honorable mission? Begin by asking yourself three questions: 1. What would I do if I knew I could not fail? 2. What would I really like to do with the only life I have? 3. What cause could I connect with that I'd be willing to die for?

Find God's answer to these questions in your life and you will move from success to significance. | ROBERT H. SCHULLER

SUNSET, TOPSAIL BEACH, FLORIDA, USA

*Let your worry drain out
and let God's peace flow in.*

ROBERT H. SCHULLER

June

FANTOME ISLAND, QUEENSLAND, AUSTRALIA

Heavenly GPS

"'Who can hide in secret places so that I cannot see them?' declares the Lord. 'Do not I fill heaven and earth?'"

JEREMIAH 23:24

Saltwater fishing has long been a passion of mine. And yet, I find there is still something very intimidating about the vastness of the Pacific Ocean. Fortunately, when I leave home port to go fishing, my boat is equipped with the modern miracle of GPS (Global Positioning System). No matter how far I purposely go in my boat, or am accidentally carried by winds or currents when the motors are off, my GPS knows exactly where I am and how to get me back home.

GPS reminds me of the "all-seeing eye of God." I find nothing more comforting than knowing God is ever-present on my journey through life. No matter how lost I get or how far away from home I drift, he is there. He never loses track of me. And he always knows how to get me safely home.

| ROBERT A. SCHULLER

GOOSEBERRY BEACH, NEWPORT, RHODE ISLAND, USA

Beware assumptions

"The plans of the diligent lead to profit
as surely as haste leads to poverty."

PROVERBS 21:5

Virtually every decision we make includes assumptions. We assume that the chair we're sitting on is strong enough to hold us. That the food set before us is safe to eat. That the air we breathe is nontoxic. And that the hand we shake is free of disease-spreading germs. Our opinions, judgments, decisions, interpretations, perceptions, conclusions, and conflict resolutions are all based on assumptions.

Assumptions are mental observations we presume to be facts before we can prove their absolute reality. It is accepting something as the truth before it can be verified. Committing to a viewpoint before all the questions can be answered.

To live a life filled with meaning and purpose, you must learn to manage your assumptions. Challenge the assumptions that block you. Don't let negative assumptions destroy your dreams. Affirm and explore your positive assumptions to achieve your mission. | ROBERT H. SCHULLER

KATHERINE GORGE, NORTHERN TERRITORY, AUSTRALIA

Godly wisdom

*"The fear of the Lord is the beginning of wisdom;
all who follow his precepts have good understanding."*

PSALM 111:10

If you have school-age children, then you know how quickly things change in this world. Many of the things I learned in school are no longer considered true. The field of science has grown by leaps and bounds. Even Einstein's theories are being challenged. And when it comes to geography, forget it. Almost every country on the continent of Africa has changed its name over the past thirty years.

Scientific knowledge changes. Geography changes. Political systems change. But godly wisdom never changes.

The wisdom of God teaches us that "people reap what they sow" (Galatians 6:7). That "pride brings a person low, but the lowly in spirit gain honor" (Proverbs 29:23). That we are saved by grace, "not by works, so that no one can boast" (Ephesians 2:8-9).

Godly wisdom is never outdated. You can depend on it for life.

| ROBERT A. SCHULLER

STOCKMAN'S REST, FALLS CREEK, VICTORIA, AUSTRALIA

No missteps with God

"The Lord makes firm the steps of those who delight in him."

PSALM 37:23

Have you ever had someone make you a promise that was misleading? When we've been misled, it's hard to trust and follow without questioning. Unless we're following a leader who leads with integrity—we will follow a leader like *that*, anywhere!

Maybe you've been tempted to wonder if God misled you or if you heard him wrong. You may have put all of your energy and faith into a project that never came to fruition. As a result you questioned yourself *and* God—maybe even both.

But God *never* misleads! He will not lead you astray or tease you with a false hope. You can trust him to keep his word. No matter how challenging your circumstances, God will walk with you and guide you if you let him.

There are no missteps for those who follow God!

| POWER FOR LIFE BIBLE

SURF LIFESAVING BOAT, GLENELG, SOUTH AUSTRALIA, AUSTRALIA

Investing in talents

"His master replied, 'Well done, good and faithful servant!
You have been faithful with a few things; I will put you in charge
of many things. Come and share your master's happiness.'"

MATTHEW 25:21

God created you gifted with talent. He wants you to use it in the power of his Spirit. But developing talent into skills takes effort. It requires time, practice, and education to fully develop your God-given talents. As you develop and invest them, God opens doors to use them. If you hide them, ignore them, or neglect them, they will diminish and fade away.

Your talents are not to squander. If you think you don't have any, ask God to reveal them to you and show you where he wants to use them through you.

It might be making apple pies to share with shut-ins. It might be writing notes of encouragement. It might be social skills useful for inviting people to church.

Discover the power of your talents today by investing them for God's sake!

| SHEILA SCHULLER COLEMAN

WATERLOO COVERED BRIDGE, WARNER, NEW HAMPSHIRE, USA

Music of the master

"For we are God's handiwork,
created in Christ Jesus to do good works,
which God prepared in advance for us to do."

E P H E S I A N S   2 : 1 0

A young man visited a church one Sunday and heard an organ offertory being played. After the service, he asked if he might play the organ. "Oh, no—only our church organist plays that instrument," came the reply.

The young man persisted. Reluctantly, they agreed to let him play. He carefully set all the stops and then began playing the very piece that had been played during the offertory. Those who lingered after the service stopped to listen. When he finished, the onlookers applauded.

"What's your name?" the church organist asked.

"Johann Sebastian Bach," he replied. "I wrote that music!"

"To think we nearly missed hearing the *real* music because I wouldn't let the master play this instrument," she sighed.

You are an instrument of God's love. Jesus Christ is the Master. Let him make lovely music in this world through you. | ROBERT H. SCHULLER

OAK ALLEY PLANTATION, LOUISIANA, USA

Distractions

"Turn to God...
so that times of refreshing may come from the Lord."

ACTS 3:19

I once asked Mother Teresa, "If God believes in us, why don't we believe in him?"

"Distractions," she replied.

Talk about distractions. You should see my mailbox. It's full. The junk mail is mixed in with bills to be paid, invitations to accept, letters from friends, thank-you notes, final notices for subscriptions, and political propaganda. And you never know when a letter with a check or a chance to win a million dollars will show up!

I talk about taking time for prayer and Bible reading—but I have to answer the mail. I absolutely can't ignore it. They might turn off my lights.

God doesn't send me checks or final notices. He's not in the stuff.

Distractions! Don't be so afraid of missing out on life that you miss the only thing that really matters. Take time for God. | ROBERT H. SCHULLER

WILDFLOWERS, LLANO, TEXAS, USA

A word of encouragement

*"Encourage one another...
and the God of love and peace will be with you."*

2 CORINTHIANS 13:11

En-*courage*-ment: Putting courage into the heart of someone who is dis-*couraged* (at risk of losing courage, heart, and giving up).

Who is the best suited for giving an encouraging word?

Most people are not cut from the courage cloth. Maybe you are someone who struggles to find the courage to step out in faith. As a result of your own struggle, you become the perfect person to give an encouraging word. You can relate! You have been there, too!

The blessing that accompanies giving a word of encouragement is that, in the process, you frequently find you have encouraged yourself. God is the source of courage. God is the reason you can continue to believe. He is the Word. Become his encourager! Spread the word!

| SHEILA SCHULLER COLEMAN

LOWER POTATO RIVER FALLS, WISCONSIN, USA

Short-circuited by shame?

"Those who receive God's abundant provision of grace and of the gift of righteousness reign in life through the one man, Jesus Christ."

ROMANS 5:17

Everybody suffers from feelings of shame. We can all think of instances where we would love to turn back time and undo something we regret. Or, at least, we hope that nobody remembers or finds out about something that makes our cheeks flush red with shame.

Shame is not necessarily limited to things we've done. Some of our shame may be inherited—shame by association, family shame, professional shame. Shame short-circuits self-esteem *and*, most importantly, our relationship with God.

Love, well-being, pride, and communication cannot flow in our lives when we are short-circuited by shame. The good news is, Jesus died to forgive us, to redeem our shame and restore our relationship with God. When our shame is redeemed, we can reconnect with our Creator and salvation is only a prayer away. | SHEILA SCHULLER COLEMAN

PICKETT'S CHARGE BATTLEFIELD, GETTYSBURG, PENNSYLVANIA, USA

H-bees

"Though an army besiege me, my heart will not fear;
though war break out against me, even then I will be confident."

PSALM 27:3

My friends and I loved using the tree-house my Grandpa built for a lunch retreat away from school. Returning to class one day, I noticed a swarm of insects with a black H on their yellow backs.

"Look! H-bees! They don't sting."

"Yeah, right!"

"I'll show you." I scooped some bare-handedly into my now-empty lunch bag.

I put the bag beneath my desk, assuming the bees would stay there. Before you know it, they were swarming all over the classroom. Everyone was squealing.

It was foolish on my part to bring something that appeared harmful to class. But everyone there had needlessly succumbed to fear. When I find myself reacting like those students and teacher, I remember that I am probably afraid of a little old H-bee and that God is gathering the harmless little critters into his bare, scarred hands. | SHEILA SCHULLER COLEMAN

SECOND BEACH, OLYMPIC NATIONAL PARK, WASHINGTON, USA

Decide to be happy

"A happy heart makes the face cheerful."

PROVERBS 15:13

One day I was driving down the freeway and noticed a bumper sticker on the back of a car that said, "Happiness is being single." I looked at that and thought, *That's right–happiness is being single. I remember when I was single–boy, was I happy.*

Then I thought, *Wait a minute, Robert–you're married!* Then I thought, *Well, I'm married and I'm still happy. Oh–happiness must be being married.*

What I learned that day is that happiness isn't a state of being. Happiness is a conscious decision you and I make as individuals. We each decide if we're going to be happy or unhappy. And that's true in every area of life.

Don't wait for your life to change so you can find happiness. Decide to be happy today! | ROBERT A. SCHULLER

ISLAND ARCH, VICTORIA, AUSTRALIA

Still the storms of stress

*"They...asked each other, 'Who is this?
Even the wind and the waves obey him!'"*

MARK 4:41

When a treacherous storm dangerously tossed around their tiny fishing boat, the disciples came to Jesus and frantically woke him. Jesus got up, put out his hands, and ordered the winds to be still and the waves to subside. The wind died down completely. Peace was restored. Then he turned to his disciples and asked, "Why are you so afraid? Where is your faith?"

There are times when all of us feel as if we are ready to drown. The pressures and stresses of life threaten to take us under. It is tempting to think at those times, *God, don't you care?*

If you lack faith, ask him for more. Call on him, for if the winds and waves obey him, how much more can he do to restore peace and calm in your life, the life of his beloved child? | POWER FOR LIFE BIBLE

KAKADU, NORTHERN TERRITORY, AUSTRALIA

Spiritual diffusers

"...my perfume spread its fragrance."

SONG OF SOLOMON 1:12

I indulged in a bamboo reed diffuser for my home. (I learned about molecular absorption and airborne diffusion in science classes.) The idea of having a lovely, delicate fragrance fill my home really appealed to me.

It occurred to me that as Christians, we can be spiritual diffusers. When we sink our spiritual roots deep into God's word, the fragrance of his love grace, and mercy are diffused through our words, smiles, and caring spirits emitting a spiritual fragrance that makes our world a sweeter place.

The fragrance we emit depends on the oils in which we are steeped. I have diffusers in grapefruit, orange spice, and lavender. But imagine the smell if the reeds were steeped in gasoline. We must carefully select the steeping medium for our spirits to ensure that the fragrance we give off is sweet.

| SHEILA SCHULLER COLEMAN

SNAPPY GUMS, WESTERN AUSTRALIA, AUSTRALIA

Never say quit!

"Continue in what you have learned and have become convinced of,
because you know those from whom you learned it."

2 TIMOTHY 3:14

As a child, I never won any academic awards in school. My teachers didn't exactly have high hopes for me. I would start each class with a bang but fizzle out toward the end. I was a daydreamer who mentally could leave the classroom during any class. And remembering to do my homework assignments was an ongoing challenge. So my early academic career was far from what anyone would call a success.

On the other hand, when I began developing a vision for my life, things changed. I graduated from an excellent college, earned a master's degree in divinity from an outstanding academic seminary, and was ordained into the Christian ministry on September 21, 1980.

I realize the initial indicators for my academic success were not good. Fortunately—nobody told me. And I guess I lacked the common sense to quit!

ROBERT A. SCHULLER

ACKERMAN COTTAGE, HILL END, NEW SOUTH WALES, AUSTRALIA

More than enough

*"I have learned the secret of being content in any and every situation,
whether well fed or hungry, whether living in plenty or in want."*

PHILIPPIANS 4:12

There are times in all of our lives when we lack sufficient time or funds. There are simply not enough minutes in the day to get everything done. Or not enough funds to make ends meet. It happens to every person and to every organization.

These are times when you will receive more than you ever thought imaginable—not only enough time or enough money or enough help from friends or volunteers, but most importantly, more than enough faith to get you through.

Lean times can be learning times if you learn to lean on God. It's during lean times that God displays his power and his loving providence. He can and will multiply your resources until you see he has somehow miraculously provided more than enough! | POWER FOR LIFE BIBLE

MILLER'S PLATFORM, BAKER'S MILL, WEST VIRGINIA, USA

Great values deliver great character

"I want to know Christ—yes, to know the power of his resurrection and participation in his sufferings, becoming like him in his death, and so, somehow, attaining to the resurrection from the dead."

PHILIPPIANS 3:10-11

Every human being—intuitively, accidentally, or intentionally—evolves into some kind of "character."

Character is the essential core that defines and describes your reputation. It is conceived and born in the arena where your life's principles are chosen. Character shapes your choices and decisions. It is the force in your personality that motivates you to set goals and manage your life to meet them. Strong character will survive any outcome.

Ralph Waldo Emerson said, "Character is that which we can do without success." What you are is more important than what you do.

In the final analysis, there are no great or non-great people. In essence we are all the same. The only difference is that some people are committed to noble and honorable values. Great values deliver great character.

| ROBERT H. SCHULLER

BOOMERANG BEACH, VICTORIA, AUSTRALIA

Night is o'er

"The night is nearly over; the day is almost here."

ROMANS 13:12

In the depth of darkness, everything feels more overwhelming. It is during these times, when it is difficult to look to the future with any semblance of hope, that you need to remember that the night is always temporary. The night will not last. It always comes to an end! If you hang in there you will live to see the sunrise and with it hope is reborn.

God is a powerful God who dispels gloom, breaks through depression, and energizes your life with the assurance that a new day is about to break on the horizon. Proclaim that hope. Cling to the promise that the night is o'er. The new day is born. Hope is alive—empowered of God—who sends the rays of his Son into the dark corners of your life, shattering the night with his light! | SHEILA SCHULLER COLEMAN

BLACK MOUNTAIN OVERLOOK, BLUE RIDGE PARKWAY, NORTH CAROLINA, USA

Fly against the wind

*"Whoever wants to be my disciple must deny themselves
and take up their cross and follow me."*

MATTHEW 16:24

Anyone who has ever watched an eagle or a giant condor soar knows what birds like these have learned: flying into the wind actually takes you higher, faster. It's why airplanes take off into the wind—the air beneath their wings gives them lift they wouldn't otherwise have. Here in Southern California we have what are known as "Santa Ana winds." They are so strong that airplanes will change direction whenever possible and fly directly into them to get the extra lift.

Next time you're tempted to take the path of least resistance or fly with the wind rather than against it, remember the soaring eagle and make a decision to fly against the wind. If you do, you'll discover this about yourself: you are stronger, can fly higher, and will be more focused than ever before.

| ROBERT A. SCHULLER

COOLAMINE COTTAGE, NEW SOUTH WALES, AUSTRALIA

Spiritual realities

*"And my God will meet all your needs
according to the riches of his glory in Christ Jesus."*

PHILIPPIANS 4:19

There are laws of nature and absolute realities that cannot be ignored. If we do, we are left to live with the inherent consequences of our choices. After all, who has jumped off a fifty-story building and lived to tell about it? The law of gravity will not be defied. And neither will God's spiritual realities.

When we fail to tithe or give back to God what is rightfully his, we frequently suffer the "natural consequences" of that choice and miss out on God's blessings.

What happens when we tithe? We discover that the ninety percent goes farther than the hundred percent ever did. That's the upside-down economy of the kingdom of God.

No matter how much we think we can't "afford" to give ten percent of our income to God, when we do, God always provides and fully satisfies our needs.

| ROBERT A. SCHULLER

CAMERON HIGHLANDS, MALAYSIA

Which seeds take root?

*"I will help you speak
and will teach you what to say."*

EXODUS 4:12

I was rehearsing my morning chapel talk, but another message kept intruding: *Challenge the kids to make Jesus Lord of their lives.*

Standing before rows of seated teenagers, I breathed an arrow prayer, asking God to use the new message. Five students stayed afterwards to pray. Another sent me a note relating her life changes after accepting Christ. Eventually I learned of one more transformed life.

Four years later at a school fundraiser, I was stunned to hear a senior speak of her life-changing decision for Christ because of my challenge during chapel. I had no idea Alex had been moved by the Spirit and had given her life to Christ that morning many years earlier.

God used me to toss out seeds of Christ's love, then guided them to receptive hearts. All it took was one little seed.

SHEILA SCHULLER COLEMAN

MABRY MILL, BLUE RIDGE PARKWAY, VIRGINIA, USA

Our Holy Spirit instinct

"But the fruit of the Spirit is love, joy, peace, patience, kindness, goodness, faithfulness, gentleness and self-control."

GALATIANS 5:22-23

Think about nature. How do salmon know when to swim upstream to spawn? How do monarch butterflies know to fly back to Monarch Bay where they are hatched? How do the swallows find their way back to San Juan Capistrano every spring?

Scientists can't explain any of these behaviors so they call them "instincts." Instincts are a special knowledge God has placed within his creatures.

We, too, have within us an innate instinct. This "instinct" is, in reality, the Holy Spirit who longs to communicate and share with us the truth we need to make every moral choice. But we must listen and obey. When we do, our life begins to demonstrate the qualities Paul refers to in Galatians 5 as "the fruit of the Spirit." And with the fruit of the Spirit in our life, we can face any moral challenge. | ROBERT A. SCHULLER

RAINBOW BRIDGE, LAKE POWELL, UTAH, USA

Jesus...full of love

"But the fruit of the Spirit is love..."

GALATIANS 5:22

Two thousand years ago nobody wanted to get within shouting distance of a leper. Leprosy was believed to be extremely contagious and victims of the disease were ostracized from the rest of society.

But Jesus reached out and touched a leper, letting him know that he was loved and valued, providing the human contact he had been denied for so long. Through his loving touch Jesus was healing the man both emotionally and physically.

Jesus entered into situations where others would not go, taking the love of God to people whom others considered to be unlovely—lepers, the lame, the blind, prostitutes, and even tax collectors.

Wherever Jesus went, he built bridges between people and between people and God. Truly he showed us how to love.

What will you do today to touch someone's life with the love of Jesus?

| ROBERT A. SCHULLER

WHITE OAK CANYON TRAIL, SHENANDOAH NATIONAL PARK, VIRGINIA, USA

Jesus...full of joy

"But the fruit of the Spirit is joy..."

GALATIANS 5:22

Somewhere people have picked up the notion that Jesus went around with a sad, stern look on his face, joyless, devoid of warmth and humor. And while it's true that Isaiah prophesied that he would be "a man of sorrows" (Isaiah 53:3), Jesus was also a man of great inner strength and joy. Certainly he was on this earth to take care of some very serious business but through it all he was joyful because he knew he was carrying out his Father's will.

The Bible describes him as "full of joy through the Holy Spirit." In John 17:13, when Jesus prayed for his disciples, he said, "I say these things while I am still in the world, so that they may have the full measure of my joy within them."

How will you share the joy of Jesus with others today?

| ROBERT A. SCHULLER

HUNTING ISLAND STATE PARK, SOUTH CAROLINA, USA

Jesus...full of peace

"But the fruit of the Spirit is peace..."

GALATIANS 5:22

I love the story Mark records in his gospel about Jesus sleeping peacefully while his disciples are frantically trying to keep their boat afloat during a terrorizing storm at sea (Mark 4:35-39).

Jesus knew that life has its stormy moments. But through it all, he kept an eternal perspective. Jesus knew he was safe and secure in his Father's love.

It's not easy to learn to rest while the storms of life assail us. Peace comes only by constantly giving our cares to God. We'd all be more peaceful if we followed the Apostle Peter's advice: "Cast all your anxiety on him because he cares for you" (1 Peter 5:7).

Jesus knew how to do that. Consequently, he could sleep in the middle of a terrible storm. We would save ourselves a lot of grief if we learned to live that way too! | ROBERT A. SCHULLER

HERON BAY, ALABAMA, USA

Jesus...full of patience

"But the fruit of the Spirit is patience..."

GALATIANS 5:22

Jesus did good for people even though he knew many of them would eventually turn against him, falsely accuse him, and demand his execution.

Think of the patience Jesus demonstrated toward Judas Iscariot; he showed love and friendship toward the man he knew would eventually betray him. And the patience Jesus demonstrated toward the other disciples who often misunderstood the nature of his mission on earth. In spite of what he taught them about serving others, they fought over who would be greatest in God's kingdom. And when Jesus needed them the most, they deserted him.

One thing you can count on in this world—people are going to let you down. That's a given. Without patience, you're going to have a very hard time in life.

Remember this: Life is not a sprint; it's a marathon.

| ROBERT A. SCHULLER

YELLOW WILDFLOWERS, WESTERN AUSTRALIA, AUSTRALIA

Jesus...full of kindness

"But the fruit of the Spirit is kindness..."

GALATIANS 5:22

The Pharisees loved to test Jesus. One day they brought a woman caught in adultery to him and asked, "In the Law, Moses commanded us to stone such a woman. What do you say?"

Jesus bent down and started writing in the dirt with his finger. When they kept on questioning him, Jesus said to them, "If any of you is without sin, let him be the first to throw a stone." One by one the crowd walked away.

Jesus showed by his actions that there are times when mercy must take precedence over judgment. Jesus didn't see the woman as an adulteress; he saw her as a human being created in God's image—as someone worthy of redemption.

Christ continually demonstrated kindness toward people, especially those society tended to write off. He asks us to do the same.

ROBERT A. SCHULLER

CHOCORUA LAKE, NEW HAMPSHIRE, USA

Jesus...full of goodness

"But the fruit of the Spirit is goodness..."

GALATIANS 5:22

Goodness puts limits on kindness. There comes a time when you have to put your foot down and say, "This is wrong, and I won't put up with it."

St. Augustine counseled, "Liberty in non-essentials, unity in essentials, and in all things, love." There are some areas where kindness must give way to judgment. And there are times when mercy is incompatible with justice and justice takes precedence over mercy.

Jesus forgave the woman taken in adultery, but exhorted her not to return to her life of sin. And there are times when we need to say, "This has to stop and it has to stop now." Jesus did not confuse kindness with tolerance of improper behavior.

Seek God's wisdom in the area of goodness. He will show you when to extend mercy and when to draw the line. | ROBERT A. SCHULLER

SARAH LEVY'S HOUSE, BOYANUP, WESTERN AUSTRALIA, AUSTRALIA

Jesus...fully faithful

"But the fruit of the Spirit is faithfulness..."

GALATIANS 5:22

Jesus knew that his calling was to go into Jerusalem where he would be put to death on the cross. Jesus tried to help his disciples understand what was coming, but they failed to grasp the reality of it. In fact, Scripture tells us that Peter took Jesus aside and scolded him for saying such things (Matthew 16:21-23).

Jesus was dreading the events that lay ahead for him, but in spite of his natural dread and fear, Jesus was determined to be faithful to the mission God had given him.

He could not be faithful to the task his Father had given him and faithful at the same time to Peter, who clearly did not want his Lord and friend to die.

Faithfulness responds obediently without losing confidence in God. Where do you need faithfulness in your life right now?

| ROBERT A. SCHULLER

MILLAA MILLAA FALLS, QUEENSLAND, AUSTRALIA

Jesus...full of gentleness

"But the fruit of the Spirit is gentleness..."

GALATIANS 5:23

Jesus was capable of great gentleness and tenderness.

Touched by the grief of Lazarus's two sisters—Mary and Martha—Jesus openly wept with these friends. I admire a man who is strong, brave, and gentle enough to cry in public. That's not an easy thing for many men to do.

Jesus had a gentle heart *and* gentle touch. So gentle, in fact, mothers brought their children to him to receive his blessing. He was a gentle, loving, caring man who truly loved children.

Jesus was also tough and rugged when it was required. It took guts to confront the religious leaders as he often did, and to go into the temple and drive out the money changers.

Jesus knew when to be gentle and when to be tough and confrontational. He is the perfect model for us to follow. | ROBERT A. SCHULLER

THE MOUNT OF TEMPTATION, HOLY LAND

Jesus...full of self-control

"But the fruit of the Spirit is self-control..."

GALATIANS 5:23

Jesus exhibited great self-control.

He was led by the Spirit into the desert, where for forty days he was tempted over and over by the devil. It's impossible to understand exactly what was going on during the temptation of Christ. All we know is that Jesus was seriously tempted, and he chose to walk away from it.

The same thing occurred when Jesus was arrested in the Garden of Gethsemane. Jesus could have called on the angels and escaped the cross. But he wouldn't do it. He was a man of great self-control, just as he was a man of great love, joy, peace, patience, kindness, goodness, faithfulness, and gentleness.

Are you ready to live a life that bears the fruit of the Spirit? With the help of God's Spirit you can live a "fruit-filled" life that can change the world!

ROBERT A. SCHULLER

ROCKPORT, MASSACHUSETTS, USA

God's care will carry you
so you can carry others!

ROBERT H. SCHULLER

July

BOUGAINVILLEA ON THE MOUNT OF BEATITUDES, SEA OF GALILEE, ISRAEL

Choose your values carefully

"God did this so that they would seek him and perhaps reach out for him and find him...For in him we live and move and have our being."

ACTS 17:27-28

The faith taught to me as a child has been the primary source of my value system. I was brought up on the Ten Commandments and the Sermon on the Mount. My values were infused with faith, hope and love because of my Judeo-Christian foundation. This faith has given me energy and enthusiasm in my life. It has motivated me to say yes to great ideas, to maintain an "I will not quit" attitude, and to have the courage to say no to the alluring values that come from a de-humanizing culture.

Positive spiritual passion is the power source that transforms people from selfish, greedy, arrogant, and duplicitous creatures into beautiful human beings who are unselfish, generous, caring, and compassionate.

Choose your values carefully. Pursue a positive faith that will boost and bless your values and shape you into a beautiful human being.

| ROBERT H. SCHULLER

MOSAIC, BETHANY, HOLY LAND

In search of morality

*"Put off your old self,
which is being corrupted by its deceitful desires."*

EPHESIANS 4:22

Take a look around and you'll see that the society in which we live increasingly seems to be missing something very important, something called morality.

Sadly, the absence of morality carries with it a terrible price tag. Broken homes. Broken hearts. Broken people. Lost ideals. Lost hopes. Lost dreams. Damaged relationships and damaged people. People in pain who thought they could slide through life doing whatever they wanted to do are now discovering the cost of living an amoral life.

So what can we do to rediscover our moral strength as individuals and as a nation? We must allow God's spirit to work within us and penetrate every fiber. We must take personal responsibility and allow the Holy Spirit to show us where change is needed. We cannot change others. We can only change ourselves...with God's help. | ROBERT A. SCHULLER

SPLIT ROCK LIGHTHOUSE, MINNESOTA, USA

A return to morality

"Just as it was in the days of Noah,
so also will it be in the days of the Son of Man."

LUKE 17:26

Recently I was waiting in line to buy a movie ticket and overheard a conversation taking place in front of me between two teenage girls. They were using language that would make a Marine blush. I was embarrassed for them but figured that because they hear people around them talk like that, they probably think it's an accepted part of ordinary conversation.

Some might say, "Oh, come on, it's only words." But the words we use are an important indication of who we are as people. Language that is cheap, shallow, and laced with obscenity is a reflection of cheap, shallow, and obscene lives.

One might think that the answer to our deteriorating moral code of conduct is to pass more laws. I'm afraid not. Only hearts changed by Jesus can return society to a place of moral civility. | ROBERT A. SCHULLER

CAMELS AT SUNSET, ABU DHABI, UAE

Spiritually fit

"To him who is able to keep you from stumbling and to present you before his glorious presence without fault and with great joy... to [him] be glory, majesty, power and authority...now and forevermore!"

JUDE 24-25

One of the Schuller grandchildren recently graduated from the police academy. He knew when he went into the academy he would face hundreds of push-ups, running miles in the heat of the day, even boxing matches against his training officers. He didn't look at the academy as a way to get in shape. No! He took over a year to get in shape *before* he applied to the academy. So, on the first day, even though it was grueling, he was in shape.

The same is true for our spiritual lives. God didn't promise life would be a cakewalk if we follow him. The more effective we are for Christ, the more opposition we can expect—from spiritual and human foes. We need to be spiritually fit if we are going to fight the good fight and *win!* | POWER FOR LIFE BIBLE

JOHN CAMERON, URQUHART CASTLE, SCOTLAND

Everyday heroes

*"Do good, O Lord, to those who are good,
to those who are upright in heart."*

PSALM 125:4

When my oldest grandson, Jason, was eleven years old, he came into my office and noticed a framed picture of me propped against the wall. "That's a nice picture of you, Grandpa," he noted. "Why isn't it hanging on the wall?"

"Because," I responded, "it was given to me and I haven't decided where to hang it yet."

"I know where you could hang it," he offered, "...in my bedroom. Because Grandpa, you're my hero."

We all need heroes. Heroes are all around us. They're in our classrooms, doctor's offices, and hospital corridors. They patrol our streets, fight fires, and secure our borders. They serve, protect, preserve...so we can continue to enjoy the many freedoms we often take for granted.

Stop for a minute and remember the heroes who've been part of your life. Thank God for them. Then aspire to be one! | ROBERT H. SCHULLER

SAND DUNES, TAL MOREEB, ABU DHABI, UAE

From zero to hero

"Even if you have been banished to the most distant land under the heavens, from there the Lord your God will gather you and bring you back."

DEUTERONOMY 30:4

Pee Wee Kirkland was destined to become one of the great basketball stars of the 1970s. But rather than enjoy a starring role on the basketball court, he spent eleven of the next eighteen years in federal penitentiaries, convicted for selling drugs and evading taxes.

"I realized how wrong I was and knew that God expected better of me," Pee Wee admits.

After his release from prison, Pee Wee made good on his commitment to improve himself and make a difference. He started a basketball program for kids in Harlem and later became the basketball coach for an exclusive prep school in New York where he not only built a winning basketball program, but also taught kids what it means to have a dream and the desire to work for it.

Get rid of your "zero" by becoming someone's hero.

| ROBERT H. SCHULLER

RAINBOW, ALICE SPRING, AUSTRALIA

War and peace

*"Grace and peace be yours in abundance
through the knowledge of God and of Jesus our Lord."*

2 PETER 1:2

Not all wars are waged on a battlefield with bombs and bullets. Some are wars of words waged between husbands and wives who have forgotten how to love each other. Others are waged in struggles between parents and children, as rivalries and resentments between brothers and sisters, or as squabbles among friends. The cost of these wars is always high. The price of peace never comes cheap.

As long as men and women do not have peace inside of them—the peace that only God can give—there will be wars of one kind or another. But peace is possible through faith in God and the power and presence of the indwelling Holy Spirit.

Surrender your "war" to God. Let his Spirit take control. And the peace of God that surpasses human understanding will guard your heart and give you peace. | ROBERT A. SCHULLER

MAHAWONG DAY CARE CENTER, THAILAND

Your positive identity

"How precious to me are your thoughts, God!
How vast is the sum of them!"

PSALM 139:17

When Isaac emerged from Abraham's shadow after being esteemed "the child of the promise" for so many years, he appeared to be a weak, passive man. Much of his family life and character was unimpressive.

But it is important to see what God saw in Isaac. He was not a charismatic personality or a perfect man, but Isaac was chosen by God to be part of the family line and fulfillment of God's purposes and a foreshadowing of the sacrifice of God's son, Jesus.

You, too, may feel that you are ordinary or merely average. But as God's child, you are important to him and directly linked to the fulfillment of his purposes. Learn to see yourself through God's eyes and you will discover your positive identity! If God thinks you're special—you are!

| POWER FOR LIFE BIBLE

CRAIG'S HUT, VICTORIA, AUSTRALIA

God's perspective

*"From the ends of the earth I call to you...
lead me to the rock that is higher than I."*

PSALM 61:2

When I was thirteen, my father and I built a small cabin in the mountains near Moonridge, California. We spent many wonderful times there together. One summer when I was sixteen I was looking out the cabin window at the surrounding mountain peaks and decided I would climb to the top of the highest one. I put on my tennis shoes and began the ascent. After a harder-than-expected climb, I reached the top only to discover it was merely a peak hiding the real summit from my vantage point in the cabin. So I started up a different peak. Same thing—it was another smaller peak behind which loomed the largest one, the true summit.

Life is a lot like that. We often cannot see the next peak God has for us until we are willing to climb the one closest to us. | ROBERT A. SCHULLER

INTERNATIONAL VISITOR CENTRE, CRYSTAL CATHEDRAL, CALIFORNIA, USA

Your family name

*"See what great love the Father has lavished on us,
that we should be called children of God! And that is what we are!"*

1 JOHN 3:1

When I purchase something with a credit card or use my driver's license for identification purposes, I'm frequently asked whether I'm related to my father.

"Are you your father's son?" I'm asked.

I always wonder—*well, who else's son could I possibly be?*

"Are you related to Robert Schuller?"

"I *am* Robert Schuller," I say, pointing to the name on the driver's license or credit card.

"No, I mean the guy up at the cathedral."

Once we get the matter straightened out, I'm always happy and proud to tell them that yes, I am related to the guy up at the cathedral.

How about you? Do you proudly and gladly wear the name of God? There's no better, stronger, more powerful family name on earth.

| ROBERT A. SCHULLER

HAVASU FALLS, SUPAI, ARIZONA, USA

God is at work in you

"God works in you...to fulfill his good purpose."

PHILIPPIANS 2:13

Wow! You don't have to do this by yourself! How reassuring to know that it is God at work in you. There is nothing more powerful than God himself working through you. And there is no more trustworthy assurance!

God gives you his will—his desires, his purpose, his plan for your life.

God gives you his power—his abilities, his courage, and his ideas to achieve his purposes.

Embrace God's promise. Let it fuel your dreams! Rest on his assurance. Go forth asking and letting him use you today!

| SHEILA SCHULLER COLEMAN

LONG JETTY, NEW SOUTH WALES, AUSTRALIA

Derailed by fear?

"Come near to God and he will come near to you."

JAMES 4:8

God longs to be close to us. He loves you. You are his child, his precious creation. When you feel distant from him, it is not because God has moved. It's because you have pulled away from him, you have broken your connection with him. One way your connection with God gets broken is through fear...of not being good enough...of him loving others more...of having too little faith. Myriads of fears can derail your relationship with God.

The antidote to fear is faith. Flexing faith power requires making a choice. It is choosing to believe even when feelings of fear threaten to choke out your faith.

Choose to believe in a forgiving God. Choose to believe in a loving God. Choose to believe that God who created you—with your fears—can restore your faith in him. | SHEILA SCHULLER COLEMAN

TINTAGEL, CORNWALL, UK

God is bigger!

*"For your ways are in full view of the Lord,
and he examines all your paths."*

PROVERBS 5:21

If your God-given dream is facing a major challenge, it's time to ask God what he wants you to do. Follow his lead, no matter how silly it might sound. Think of some of the most successful people you know, and then think how they might have felt when they first started out. Do you ever think Walt Disney might have felt silly building an entire enterprise on a cartoon mouse? How about building an international ministry from the snack-bar roof of a drive-in theatre? Do you think Ronald Reagan might have felt silly telling Gorbachev to tear down the wall of Berlin? (Why would he say yes after years of saying no?)

What is your challenge? What is your setback? God is bigger! Take a stand for him today and allow him to tear down the walls. He is able!

| POWER FOR LIFE BIBLE

ELEPHANTS, MT. KILIMANJARO, TANZANIA

Tap in to God's power

"Your hand will guide me, your right hand will hold me fast."

PSALM 139:10

If you knew you could make a positive difference, what would it be? Imagine yourself doing that with God's hand holding yours, leading the way. What obstacles are you afraid you will encounter? Is it your age? Is it your lack of experience? If so, there are probably others elsewhere who were in your shoes at one point in their lives, but they were able to overcome a similar obstacle. Isn't God big enough to help you take the necessary steps to forge ahead?

Think of all the people who would be helped if you said yes to your calling. Now, think of all the people who won't be helped if you say no. Finally, tap into God's power. Ask him to fill you with his Spirit. When you do, don't be surprised if your life lights up with enthusiasm!

POWER FOR LIFE BIBLE

YOUNG WOMAN, AL HAMRA LAKE, EGYPT

My weakness, God's strength

"Strengthen the feeble hands, steady the knees that give way."

ISAIAH 35:3

My mother is always on call for me. One morning when I felt completely inadequate for a task, I phoned Mom.

"I can't do this, Mom. I lack the skills and innate abilities the project requires. This dream needs someone fearless. I'm too reluctant to sell myself or my projects."

"Well, Sheila," Mom said, "that just means your dream is God-given. God will only give you a dream that demands his help so he gets the credit while building your faith. If it's something you can do all by yourself, you don't need God. A dream that is too big for you drives you to your knees, which is exactly where he wants you."

Mother knows best! When I feel inadequate I put my trust in God. I grow spiritually and watch God in action. And I wouldn't miss that for the world!

| SHEILA SCHULLER COLEMAN

THE WAILING WALL, JERUSALEM

True prayer

"Let us draw near to God with a sincere heart."

HEBREWS 10:22

You probably know and can recite from memory The Lord's Prayer, which ends, "For Thine is the kingdom, and the power, and the glory forever." But I wonder if you fully understand what that sentence means?

Pretend you are in a boat. You paddle your way to the sandy shore until you are within reach of the beach where you throw down the anchor. When the anchor digs into the sand, you pull on the rope until you hear the sound of gravel crunching under the bottom of the boat and you step out onto solid ground. You haven't moved the beach to the boat; you've moved the boat to the beach.

Likewise, the purpose of prayer is not to move God to you, it is to draw you closer to God so your life can fit into his plans. | ROBERT H. SCHULLER

NORTH END, REFUGE COVE, WILSONS PROMONTORY, VICTORIA, AUSTRALIA

Cell by cell

"Jesus of Nazareth...went around doing good and healing."

ACTS 10:38

My second son, Christopher, had severe asthma as a baby. My fourth son, Nicholas, had an immune deficiency that resulted in frequent bouts of pneumonia. I prayed every night asking God to heal both boys.

Christopher was nearly one year old when the allergist asked me about the dosage of his asthma medications. I explained he hadn't taken any medication for months, thinking he had outgrown the asthma. Christopher never suffered from asthma again.

Similarly, Nicholas gradually improved until one day he no longer chronically needed antibiotics. Both boys had been healed gradually.

We often expect instant miracles when we pray. God's principle of healing is usually cell by cell over time. It's imperceptible, often happening slowly and invisibly. One day you wake up to recognize there's healing. God has done a miracle! | SHEILA SCHULLER COLEMAN

SOUTH END, REFUGE COVE, WILSONS PROMONTORY, VICTORIA, AUSTRALIA

Dump your hang-ups

*"My flesh and my heart may fail,
but God is the strength of my heart and my portion forever."*

PSALM 73:26

Everyone has an "Achilles Heel"—a vulnerable spot that, if aggravated, can really send a person plummeting into anger, depression, or hopelessness. Perhaps you've learned to manage your vulnerabilities—your hang-ups. Or maybe you haven't. So when outside stressors come, your hang-ups" feel like millstones tied around your neck, pulling you with great force to rock bottom.

Today, if you're feeling as if you cannot go any lower, as if there's no hope, as if your future holds nothing but pain and grief and fear, then it's time to stop and look straight into the face of God and cry: "God, I'm powerless. I believe you are all-powerful. Today I'm relinquishing control of my life to you. Do what you must."

Take these steps and watch what God can and will do in your life.

| ROBERT A. SCHULLER

CANNONBALL, TASMANIA, AUSTRALIA

Admit your need

"Now to him who is able to do immeasurably more than all we ask or imagine according to his power that is at work within us."

EPHESIANS 3:20

Methodist missionary E. Stanley Jones used to conduct "ashrams" (times of spiritual growth and development). He would begin each ashram by asking people to answer this question in writing: "What is your need today?" And he would add, "Be honest. No one will see what you've written."

It was inevitable—as people were thinking and praying and writing someone would say, "Brother Stanley, I don't have a need. What do you write down if you don't have a need?"

"If you think you don't have a need, then *that's* your need!" Brother Stanley would reply.

Why are we so reluctant to admit our need? I think we are afraid that people will reject us or that we'll feel embarrassed.

But remember this: The only thing you have to fear is what results from hiding your lack, your need, or your poverty. | ROBERT H. SCHULLER

GAIL'S LOUNGEROOM, QUAMBY BROOK, TASMANIA, AUSTRALIA

Spread the light

"Let your light shine before others."

MATTHEW 5:16

You go into a large room that is completely void of light. You take a tiny match from your pocket. You strike it. Light pierces the darkness. It casts a glow deep into the room.

Although light is always stronger than darkness, you may still be hesitant to let your light shine. Why are you so timid about striking a match in the dark? If the odds of victory are overwhelmingly on your side, then shouldn't you be more en-*couraged* to light a light? Why do you tend to hide your light under a bushel? How much darkness is left unchallenged because you have hidden your God-given light?

Let your light shine every day...through a smile, a card, or an encouraging word. | SHEILA SCHULLER COLEMAN

AMBOSEILI NATIONAL PARK, KENYA

Snipe hunt

*"I am sending you to them to open their eyes
and turn them from darkness to light, and from the power of Satan to God,
so that they may receive forgiveness of sins
and a place among those who are sanctified by faith in me."*

ACTS 26:17-18

Many childhood summers included mountain visits as camper and counselor. I feel God's presence in the mountains. They became my spiritual home.

This is surprising considering the summer a "trickster" camper convinced me I could become a camp heroine by catching a snipe.

I practiced calling snipe all afternoon. After dinner I shivered on a cold rock in the dark woods, tapping my paper bag "trap" while whistling for snipe. Finally, a friend rescued me from being "had." I didn't feel heroic, only foolish.

I wonder if some people fear trusting God lest they find at the end of life that none of this "Jesus story" *is* actually true. Dad says, "Better that than the alternative!"—not believing in Jesus then discovering in the end that it *is* true. Believing gains heaven.

I'll be foolish for Jesus any day! | SHEILA SCHULLER COLEMAN

ROAD TO CAPE LEVEQUE, WESTERN AUSTRALIA, AUSTRALIA

The trust test

"Trust in the Lord with all your heart…
in all your ways submit to him,
and he will make your paths straight."

PROVERBS 3:5-6

Trust releases a tremendous power within us. A trusting person is a persistent person. A person who doesn't trust is a skeptic. And skeptics tend to give up quickly.

When you begin to trust God, you discover real power. You come to the realization that God believes in you and trusts you, and recognizing this you begin to trust yourself. That's when God begins to release real power in your life—the power of self-confidence, the power to trust others, and the power to trust the ideas God gives you. When someone trusts you, they help bring out the best in you. God trusts you because you are his child; you are created in his image.

Next time you're short on trust, repeat this positive affirmation: "I am God's child. I trust him and he trusts me." | ROBERT H. SCHULLER

CLAY VESSELS, IRANIAN SOUK, ABU DHABI , UAE

Multiplied resources

"You are the God who performs miracles;
you display your power among the peoples."

PSALM 77:14

Elisha traded a life of luxury for a life of living on the providence of God. One day Elisha met a distraught widow who had no money to repay a lender. She begged Elisha to help her when the lender demanded payment of her sons as slaves. All she had was a few drops of olive oil.

Elisha instructed her to gather empty jars from her neighbors—as many as she could find—and to begin filling the pots with her oil. Miracle of miracles, the oil kept flowing until every jar in her house was full. Then Elisha told her to sell the oil and pay off her debts and live on what was left.

Where do you need to see God multiply your resources? Will you trust him to provide everything, and even more than you need?

| POWER FOR LIFE BIBLE

SILVERSMITH INLAYING MOTHER-OF-PEARL, ABU DHABI, UAE

Life's puzzles

*"The eyes of the Lord range throughout the earth
to strengthen those whose hearts are fully committed to him."*

2 CHRONICLES 16:9

Jigsaw puzzles have become an annual vacation tradition for our family. Through the years we've had access to a condominium in a lovely beach setting where we go to unwind for a couple of weeks each year. There we always find a vast supply of difficult jigsaw puzzles just waiting for us to tackle as a family.

It isn't long before we pull out a puzzle and dump it on a table. And there it sits, multiplying like some multi-cell organism, until we finally snap the last piece into place. When the puzzle is done, whether it takes a day or a week, it goes back in the box and we're on to the next puzzle.

Life is like that. It's the endless supply of puzzles that makes life challenging and exciting. Life is enhanced by the puzzles we're called to solve.

| ROBERT A. SCHULLER

THE TWELVE APOSTLES, VICTORIA, AUSTRALIA

From success to significance

"They help each other and say to their companions,
'Be strong!'"

ISAIAH 41:6

What good is success if it hurts others? We can all think of examples of someone who succeeded in creating havoc or hurt. If others aren't helped, what good is success? The world is too needy to spend your life aiming high but helping nobody!

What helpful thing could you do with your life? Where is there a need? How could you make a significant dent on the hurt that is rampant in our world?

Even if you are housebound, you can participate in an online suicide prevention network. Don't feel qualified? They'll train you! Not housebound? There are soup kitchens in almost every city desperate for people to serve the hungry who don't know where their next meal is coming from.

Pray today: Lord, show me where you need me most! I will say yes.

| SHEILA SCHULLER COLEMAN

BUSHFIRES, WEIPA, QUEENSLAND, AUSTRALIA

Burnt to a crisp

"All the days ordained for me were written in your book
before one of them came to be."

PSALM 139:16

My parents left me alone one summer to study Physics.

On Sunday I sliced and sprinkled a tomato with Parmesan for broiling. Coming home from class the following day, I planned a repeat of that until suddenly, I thought: *Did I eat yesterday's slices? Could it be? Nah!*

When I opened the oven minutes later, I discovered that my tomato was nothing but a pile of ashes. The broiler had been on for twenty-four hours. Thank God the house hadn't burned down!

Although I felt old enough to be left alone, and my parents thought me mature enough, I obviously was not.

Today I realize no one is made to go it alone, even singles. Jesus is stronger than a brother or father. He wants the central role in your life. Invite him in. You will never be alone. | SHEILA SCHULLER COLEMAN

SUNRISE, NORTH CURL CURL, NEW SOUTH WALES, AUSTRALIA

Our most powerful antidote

"...so that your faith might not rest on human wisdom,
but on God's power."

I CORINTHIANS 2:5

I once witnessed a native in Thailand milking the poison from a cobra. It was incredible how this native would taunt and tease the cobra until the head went up and the snake began to hiss and throw himself to strike the man with deadly poison. But the native knew exactly how to grab the cobra at the back of the neck and squeeze under its jaws. First the mouth opened and the two ivory fangs were bared, then he would press the glands and the drops of white liquid poison would ooze out into a small vial. Three hours after being milked, the cobra would have venom again—enough to kill someone.

It's the same with negative thoughts. You and I constantly have to milk the cobra of our minds. And our most powerful antidote is the positive wisdom of God's word. | ROBERT H. SCHULLER

BECALMED, ARNHEM LAND, NORTHERN TERRITORY, AUSTRALIA

Understanding God's will

"He reached down from on high and took hold of me;
he drew me out of deep waters."

PSALM 18:16

People often ask, "Why does a loving God allow so much pain and suffering in this world?"

I believe God has an *intentional* will and an *interventional* will.

God doesn't plan for you to get cancer, or for your husband to leave, or your child to be abused. That's *not* God's plan. God's *intentional* will is for you to be born, enjoy childhood, develop your talents, become a creative, constructive force in society, and build a wonderful world.

But we mess it up. Other people do too. So does the world...and the devil. Then God has to deal with the mess. Here's where his *intentional* will shifts to his *interventional* will. He says to those broken in body and spirit, "What can we do now that this has happened? Let's work on it together. We'll bring some good out of it." | ROBERT H. SCHULLER

HOPETOUN FALLS, VICTORIA, AUSTRALIA

See it, be it!

"For everyone who asks receives; those who seek find;
and to those who knock, the door will be opened."

MATTHEW 7:8

Dr. Viktor Frankl used this definition for LOVE: "Love is wanting to uncover the potential in people."

That's how God loves you! It's how Jesus loves you! He wants to uncover the possibilities within you.

The person you see in your mind is the person you will be. Let me illustrate this point with a story. The famous artist, Michelangelo, had a huge chunk of marble that had been cast aside by sculptor after sculptor because it was too long and narrow. When asked what it was for, he said, "I see David." He chiseled and carved, and chiseled and carved until his work was finally finished. And there it was—the image of David. Michelangelo saw the potential in the marble, so created David in it.

Ask God to reveal the wonderful person he's hidden in you.

| ROBERT H. SCHULLER

MOUNT RUSHMORE, BLACK HILLS NATIONAL FOREST, SOUTH DAKOTA, USA

Find a need and fill it

"Let others...see your good deeds
and glorify your Father in heaven."

MATTHEW 5:16

A daily prayer in the Schuller household was, "Lord, what are you up to today? I want to be a part of it!"

Perhaps that's why the entire Schuller family is involved in ministry today—in one form or another. God will very likely show you many, many opportunities to serve him as the result of praying in this way. It has a way of opening your eyes to all the Lord is doing and how much he needs your help. In fact, you will see more opportunities than you alone are capable of getting involved in.

If you dare to pray this prayer, be prepared for God to reveal a need. Be prepared to meet that need, and be prepared to say yes. Try it at least once. Your life—and the lives of others—will be forever changed.

SHEILA SCHULLER COLEMAN

CARTER SHIELDS CABIN, GREAT SMOKY MOUNTAINS NATIONAL PARK, TENNESSEE, USA

Creative packaging

"Jesus said to him, 'Today salvation has come to this house…
For the Son of Man came to seek and to save what was lost.'"

LUKE 19:9-10

Nick and Lucy Della Valle are little people. Crystal Cathedral members and former staff, each has a big heart and a giant faith in a small but powerful package. It is the package that people notice first. And God had a plan to use the package to get people's attention.

Nick and Lucy left our staff a few years back because they were called to walk thirty-three hundred miles—one hundred miles for every year Christ walked on earth—to raise the awareness that anybody can do anything through Christ!

Big or little, rich or poor, saint or sinner, Jesus can use you if you let him. It might be as big an assignment as walking across the U.S. or as simple as e-mailing encouraging notes to someone who needs a positive connection. Whoever you are—God can use you! | POWER FOR LIFE BIBLE

SIESTA BEACH, SARASOTA, FLORIDA, USA

God doesn't say "No."
He does say "Grow!"

ROBERT H. SCHULLER

August

BRIGHTON BEACH HUTS, VICTORIA, AUSTRALIA

The joy of belonging

"You also are among those...who are called to belong to Jesus Christ."

ROMANS 1:6

There is tremendous joy in belonging. I have the joy of belonging to the Schuller family and the joy of belonging to the human race. More importantly, I have the tremendous joy of belonging to the family of God.

There are many people who are in a place where they don't have joy in their families and can't find joy in the human race. They may be in a situation or place in life where there isn't much joy. But there is one place I know where everyone can find joy—and that is in the family of God.

The Apostle Paul says in Romans 1:6, "You are among those who are called to belong to Jesus Christ." You may not find joy in belonging anywhere else, but I promise you—there is great joy in belonging to Jesus Christ.

| ROBERT A. SCHULLER

HEART REEF, GREAT BARRIER REEF, QUEENSLAND, AUSTRALIA

This time with feeling!

"For I am convinced that neither death nor life, neither angels nor demons,
neither the present nor the future, nor any powers, neither height nor depth,
nor anything else in all creation, will be able to separate us from
the love of God that is in Christ Jesus our Lord."

ROMANS 8:38-39

As usual, our family was seated around the family dinner table. Dad asked me to read from the Bible, which was part of our family routine. As I read, Dad suddenly interrupted me, "Read it again, Sheila. This time with feeling!"

Sigh! He wanted more feeling. I should have known that was coming. Taking a big breath, I dove into the passage again and this time read it with feeling.

Not only did that lesson prepare me for drama and effective presentations throughout my schooling and my life, but when I read the Bible with feeling, I see the depth, the beauty, and even the drama of God's word.

Try it. Read today's verse aloud with feeling. Get in the habit of doing it. It will bring great depth to your appreciation of God's word.

| SHEILA SCHULLER COLEMAN

MASAI TRIBESMEN, TANZANIA

You are God's treasure

"The Lord has chosen you to be his treasured possession."

DEUTERONOMY 14:2

In three short parables about hidden treasure, pearls and lost coins, Jesus defines just how much he values you. God paid the ultimate price *for you*—he purchased you with the life of his own Son!

Do you value yourself as much as God values you? Do you see yourself as a treasure for whom God would give his Son's life?

Unfortunately, most of us don't. We devalue the treasure that God values above all else. Some of us even trash God's treasure. Whether it's an attempt to be humble, a lack of appreciation for how God made us, or just downright contempt for who we are—the truth is, low self-esteem muddies the treasure.

True humility is not thinking less of yourself—it's thinking more of God. You're the child of the King. You're God's valued treasure. Live like it today!

| POWER FOR LIFE BIBLE

ELEPHANT, ZAMBEZI RIVER, ZIMBABWE

Ordinary or extraordinary

"With your help I can advance against a troop;
with my God I can scale a wall."

2 SAMUEL 22:30

You've probably heard stories told about incidents where average human beings exhibit almost super-human strength in emergency situations. Two people are working on an automobile. One is underneath the car. The jack collapses and the car falls, pinning one of the men beneath the vehicle. The other man finds himself lifting the car, rescuing his coworker from certain, crushing death. Where did he get the strength of a giant to rescue his friend?

Do you know how strong you are? None of us really does—until we come face to face with a situation that demands we tap into a hidden potential and supernatural power that transcends what's normally human.

How can we do this? With big-thinking belief and unfathomable faith in an extraordinary God. | ROBERT H. SCHULLER

THE TWELVE APOSTLES, VICTORIA, AUSTRALIA

A work in progress

"Let perseverance finish its work so that you may be mature and complete, not lacking anything."

JAMES 1:4

I worked part-time as a tour guide for a travel agency while in college. One of the places I traveled that captured my interest was the art museum in Florence, Italy, that houses Michelangelo's sculpture of David.

As the guide led us down the hallway of the museum, I glanced down a corridor and noticed a huge chunk of crudely shaped marble. It was a piece of sculpture Michelangelo never completed. And flanking the sides of the hallway were other incomplete works of his, too. I was fascinated by his "yet to-be," "what-if," "could-have-been" pieces. The perfection of Michelangelo's David was overshadowed by the embryonic potential that lay dormant in those formless rocks.

Maybe that's how you're feeling. I have good news for you. God sees the work of art buried deep inside you. Be patient. God isn't finished with you yet!

| ROBERT A. SCHULLER

THE SKILLION, TERRIGAL, NEW SOUTH WALES, AUSTRALIA

The size of your thinking

"I can do all this through him who gives me strength."

PHILIPPIANS 4:13

One of my hobbies is raising Japanese koi fish.

People have asked me, "Why are some of the fish so big and others so little?" Great question! If a koi fish lives in a small tank, it will never grow longer than two or three inches. In a larger pond, however, these fish can grow up to ten inches long. In ponds the size of mine, they will get to be a foot-and-a-half in length. But if they live in a huge lake where they can swim and stretch, they can grow up to three feet long. The size of the pond determines the size of the fish.

Similarly, little ideas in little-thinking minds produce little achievements. But little ideas embraced by big-thinking minds, often produce enormous achievements. The size of your thinking will determine the ultimate outcome of your idea! | ROBERT H. SCHULLER

KINGS OF THE SERENGETI, TANZANIA

Choose your words carefully

"Do not let any unwholesome talk come out of your mouths,
but only what is helpful for building others up according to their needs,
that it may benefit those who listen."

E P H E S I A N S   4 : 2 9

During the French Revolution, the king and queen were both beheaded and the crown prince was left orphaned. There was talk about beheading the prince, too, when someone protested, "Don't behead him; you'll only send his soul to heaven and that's too good for royalty! Turn him over to Old Meg. She will teach him vile, filthy words and his soul will be dammed forever."

So they turned the prince over to this wretched woman of the streets who tried to get the prince to repeat all kinds of profanity. But he adamantly refused! "I will not say it!" the prince screamed. "I was born to be a king and I will not say it!"

YOU were born to be a prince under the kingship of Christ. So choose your words carefully. Let your words be both affirming and encouraging. That's kingly! | ROBERT H. SCHULLER

GIRAFFES, SIR BANI YAS ISLAND, ABU DHABI, UAE

The bitter truth about gossip

"The perverse stir up dissension,
and gossips separate close friends."

PROVERBS 16:28

None of us likes to have untrue stories told about us. But have you thought about the harm that comes when you participate in gossip? By putting others down, you feel superior—even if it's for only a fleeting and ultimately unsatisfactory moment. Think of it like chocolate. It tastes good in the mouth, but the regret you feel when you go to button your pants verifies the truth that you should have resisted the temptation to indulge.

The counterpart to gossip is affirming, expressing, and displaying appreciation and affection for others. The best way to resist chocolate is to substitute something healthy in its place. The same is true about gossip. Use affirming language as a healthy substitute.

Discover the power of saying something nice about somebody. Not only will it change the other person's life, it will change yours as well.

POWER FOR LIFE BIBLE

HACKBERRY GENERAL STORE, ROUTE 66, ARIZONA, USA

Bitter butter

*"See to it that no one falls short of the grace of God
and that no bitter root grows up to cause trouble and defile many."*

HEBREWS 12:15

Our family made annual treks from California to Iowa every summer to visit family.

Usually Mom prepared our meals at a rest stop. So, it was a rare treat when we got to order breakfast in a restaurant. Plates arrived towering with pancakes—mine with succulent blueberries. We liberally poured melted butter and maple syrup over our stacks of pancakes from little pitchers. Yuck! Almost as one we spat out our mouthfuls.

Dad called the waitress over. She scanned our plates, examined the pitchers, and whisked everything away. Before long she returned with fresh meals and an apology, explaining that the night crew had left the garlic butter out and the morning shift had innocently warmed it.

Bitter butter destroyed our pancakes just as bitterness does life's joys. Ask Christ to replace any bitterness with the sweet taste of his forgiveness.

| SHEILA SCHULLER COLEMAN

INDIANA CABIN, INDIANA, USA

When values clash

*"Flee the evil desires of youth and pursue righteousness,
faith, love and peace...out of a pure heart."*

2 TIMOTHY 2:22

What do you do when your values clash?

Conflict between values is often not between good and bad, but between good and best. Or between mediocrity and excellence. Deciding between values when they clash is never easy. Do you focus on growing your business or build a great marriage and spend time with your kids? Do you send your child to a private school or provide better care for your elderly mother? Do you move across country for a better-paying job or get along" and stay in a community your family loves?

Commit to keeping non-negotiable values that say yes to life's positive possibilities and no to life's negative temptations and distractions. Once chosen, guard your values with your life. Set boundaries that protect and project your values.

Holding to your values will deliver to you a successful and satisfying tomorrow. | ROBERT H. SCHULLER

ANTEBELLUM MANSION, LOUISIANA, USA

The fleeting nature of things

"Watch out! Be on your guard against all kinds of greed;
life does not consist in an abundance of possessions."

LUKE 12:15

In Southern California we know how possessions can let us down. We've seen huge, multi-million-dollar homes slide down the hillsides and be dashed into pieces in the valleys below. We've watched expensive homes go up in flames during the brush-fires that occasionally sweep across our portion of the "Golden State." We've seen a single fire or mud slide wipe out a lifetime's worth of possessions once obtained at great expense.

Anyone who tries to take refuge behind a pile of things is going to wind up bitterly disappointed.

Things are destructible, perishable, fleeting. Our only refuge when possessions vanish is God. Trust him with your things.

| ROBERT A. SCHULLER

SAND DUNES, EUCLA, WESTERN AUSTRALIA, AUSTRALIA

Unexpected opportunities

*"Listen, my son, and be wise,
and keep your heart on the right path."*

PROVERBS 23:19

The Quakers were taught to pray each night before they went to sleep. And they were also taught to pray on awakening each morning to seek divine wisdom by coming up with a fresh list of what they could do that day. The new day might be a virtual repeat of the day before, but not necessarily!

The morning news comes on. An unexpected phone call interrupts. A conversation takes place that results in a new idea—and your priorities bend to accommodate it.

Providence has a way of challenging our carefully planned day with uninvited and unexpected fresh possibilities. So make a new priority list every morning. You'll be surprised at how frequently your priorities can and should be urgently, wisely, and even compassionately revised.

ROBERT H. SCHULLER

PEARLING LUGGER, BROOME, WESTERN AUSTRALIA, AUSTRALIA

Our call to action

"It is the Lord your God you must follow...
Keep his commands and obey him; serve him and hold fast to him."

DEUTERONOMY 13:4

A high school principal invited recruiters from three branches of the military to come and speak to their students. Each recruiter was given fifteen minutes to speak.

The Army recruiter spoke first...but went five minutes overtime.

The Navy recruiter spoke next. He also spoke longer than the time allotted.

Finally, it was the Marine's time to speak. But before he could say a word, the principal interrupted, telling him he only had time for a two-minute presentation.

Without saying a word, the Marine walked down the aisles, looked each student in the eye, and calmly announced: "Only two or three of you in this entire school can qualify to be a Marine." Guess which recruiter the students flocked to?

Following Jesus is a call to action. We've been called to make a positive difference in the world. Are you up to the challenge? | ROBERT A. SCHULLER

GRANGEVILLE, IDAHO, USA

God needs you

"You, Lord, reward everyone according to what they have done."

PSALM 62:12

My father used to tell the story of a preacher who came to call on a farmer and noticed how all of the corn was growing in straight, clean rows. Then he looked over at the waving acres of golden wheat and said to the farmer, "Look at the corn. Look at the wheat. Isn't it beautiful what God has done with this farm?" Nodding, the farmer replied, "Yeah, but you should have seen it when the Lord had it all by himself!"

God needs you and me to do his work. In a world where so many people need help, there's no excuse to say, "I don't make a difference." Yes you do. Your life has great value.

Stop for a minute right now and make a list of the work God wants you to do for him today. | ROBERT H. SCHULLER

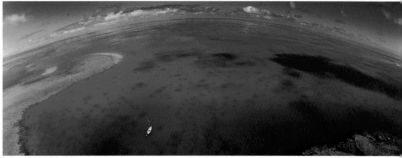

GREAT BARRIER REEF, QUEENSLAND, AUSTRALIA

Risks and rewards

"Commit your way to the Lord;
trust in him and he will do this."

PSALM 37:5

Hudson Taylor, founder of the China Inland Mission, understood the mix of faith and risk. "Unless there is an element of risk in our exploits for God, there is no need for faith."

Throughout Scripture, God appeared to ordinary people he called to do extraordinary things for him. Almost always, the person he called was afraid of what God was asking him to do. So God made a promise: "I'll do it, if you won't be afraid. But you have to trust me."

Sometimes the person said yes to God...and their world was never the same. Sometimes the person said no...and they missed out on the adventure of a risky faith with God.

People who risk nothing, do nothing, have nothing—leave nothing behind. Don't let the fear of taking risks cause you to throw away your tomorrows. Believers eventually become achievers! | ROBERT H. SCHULLER

TROPICAL PARADISE, QUEENSLAND, AUSTRALIA

Debilitated by anxiety?

"The eternal God is your refuge,
and underneath you are his everlasting arms."

DEUTERONOMY 33:27

God created you with a survival mechanism. When in danger, adrenaline increases your heart rate and respiration. This enables you to react more quickly. Known as the "flight syndrome," this protective mechanism often kicks in when you feel anxious or nervous, producing anxiety or a panic attack.

Ten percent of the population report having had a panic attack within their lifetime. (This figure is likely low due to the fact that people are reluctant to admit or slow to recognize this phenomenon). Even if you never have a panic attack, anxiety can be debilitating. It can create a wedge in your relationship with God, or it can drive you into his arms. When anxiety kicks in, flee to God. When it strikes, throw yourself into your Father's protective arms. Breathe in his love, his power, and his promise to keep you safe.

SHEILA SCHULLER COLEMAN

BROOME, WESTERN AUSTRALIA, AUSTRALIA

Facing contradictions creatively

"Through patience a ruler can be persuaded,
and a gentle tongue can break a bone."

PROVERBS 25:15

L ife is filled with contradictions. In society we are all free but living under law. We're involved but lonely. Connected but alienated. Successful but unsatisfied. Given all these social contradictions, is it any wonder we're confused, tense, and uptight?

We are routinely told things like: "Take it easy," but also "Get with it! "Be serious," but also "Relax!" "Have fun," but "Be good!" "Take a chance, but also "Take care!"

Even our clichés are contradictory. "Strike while the iron is hot"; "Haste makes waste"; "The early bird gets the worm"; and "Fools rush in where angels fear to tread."

We cannot deny the existence of contradictions nor can we ignore them Instead, we must recognize, identify, define, and deal with them; to welcome life's contradictions as places where corrections can be made. Learn to face your contradictions creatively! | ROBERT H. SCHULLER

SUNSET, PICNIC ROCKS, TASMANIA, AUSTRALIA

A spirit of gentleness

"Let your gentleness be evident to all."

PHILIPPIANS 4:5

When I was a teenager Walter Lotts, a dear family friend, gave me my first job. I walked up and down rows cutting asparagus.

I was quite impressed with Walter, one reason being that he drove a Cadillac.

One day he sent me to get something from the trunk of his Cadillac. But when I went to close the trunk, I couldn't get it to shut. I slammed it down, but it bounced back up. So I slammed it again, harder this time. It bounced open again.

Watching me with a bemused look on his face, Walter leisurely strolled over and took me by the hand.

"Always treat things like you treat a baby," he said. Then slowly, gently he pulled the trunk lid down and it locked into place.

Gentleness is pleasing to God...and people find it pleasing too.

| ROBERT A. SCHULLER

BUDGEWOI, NEW SOUTH WALES, AUSTRALIA

Reconnect to God's grace

"If we confess our sins, he is faithful and just and will forgive us our sins and purify us from all unrighteousness."

1 JOHN 1:9

Guilt always disconnects us from God. Whether it is something large or small, it matters not. Any guilt, even unreasonable, undeserved imagined guilt, can sever our connection with God, because we suddenly feel unworthy in his presence.

God is perfect. He has no guilt in him. Our guilt severs our relationship with him. The connection, even though we are wired for connectivity, is snapped in two. But God, our Great Connector, longs to be in fellowship with us. So, he sent his Son, Jesus Christ, to redeem us. Through him, our debt was paid. He washes our guilt away through his grace. All we have to do is accept the gift. Undeserved, freely given, it is as easy as saying yes to his grace. Then we can look once again in his face. We're reconnected with God! Hallelujah! | SHEILA SCHULLER COLEMAN

GENERAL SHERMAN TREE, SEQUOIA NATIONAL PARK, CALIFORNIA, USA

Wrestling with God

"Test me, Lord, and try me,
examine my heart and my mind."

PSALM 26:2

Jacob stole his older twin brother's inheritance. The result? Esau threatened to kill him and Jacob was forced to flee from his home. Jacob eluded Esau for years. But the day finally came when Jacob had to face up to what he had done. One day, Esau came after Jacob with four hundred men. The subsequent encounter with his brother marks the critical moment when God confronts Jacob and for the first time in his life, Jacob takes a hard look at himself.

With Jacob desperate to change and terrified of what he faces with Esau, God comes to him in the night. Jacob wrestles with God, refusing to let go until God blesses him.

Are you willing to be honest and wrestle with your issues without making excuses? Ask God to touch your life and change you so you can become all he made you to be. | POWER FOR LIFE BIBLE

CANNON BEACH, OREGON, USA

Freed from fear

"You will stand firm and without fear."

JOB 11:15

What are you *most* afraid of right now? What is the toughest enemy you face today? Is it the people around you? A job that confounds you? Self-doubt that surrounds you?

I believe the greatest enemy that people battle today is fear. And I'm not alone in that belief. More than a hundred years ago, author Henry David Thoreau remarked, "Nothing is so much to be feared as fear." Francis Bacon expressed that same idea two centuries earlier.

Fear saps your creativity. It wears you down. It keeps you from obtaining all the glories God has in store for you. It's a stubborn enemy. But it can be overcome. How?

Trace your fear.

Erase your fear.

Allow God to grace your fear.

Three small steps...let them lead you from fear to a lifetime of peace.

| ROBERT A. SCHULLER

AMERICAN FALLS, NIAGARA FALLS, NEW YORK, USA

Let go and let God

"Cast all your anxiety on him because he cares for you."

1 PETER 5:7

Richard Neutra, architect of the Crystal Cathedral's Tower of Hope, is well-known among architects throughout the world. One day I asked Richard, "Have you had any disappointments in life?"

"Yes, I have," he responded.

"What were they?" I asked.

He paused for a long time and finally said, "I have never received the recognition I felt I deserved from my own profession. I received a gold medal from the President of the United States. I've received gold medals from Japan, Austria, Germany, and Switzerland. But the American Institute of Architects has never recognized my work."

Richard died a few years later. And seven years after that, the American Institute of Architects gave him the gold medal.

What suffering, setback, insult, or injustice are you holding on to? Get rid of it! Give it to God! Let it go. | ROBERT H. SCHULLER

SALT LAKE , KAMBALDA, WESTERN AUSTRALIA, AUSTRALIA

A bad impression

*"The words of the reckless pierce like swords,
but the tongue of the wise brings healing."*

PROVERBS 12:18

There was a bus driver who had a female passenger that was really irritated by something. She let loose with a string of cuss words. The other passengers on the bus were shocked by her words. When the bus stopped and the angry passenger was exiting, the driver said to her, "Madame you left something behind." When she asked what it was he answered, "A very bad impression."

How do you handle upsetting situations? It is easy to let go with some profanity or anger in these kinds of situations. But let me encourage you to cultivate a skillful, sophisticated capacity to handle upsetting experiences.

Next time you are facing a negative assault, remember—you have the freedom to choose how you will react. Choose to use positive words that keep your dignity intact as well as those around you. | ROBERT H. SCHULLER

SALT LAKE , KAMBALDA, WESTERN AUSTRALIA, AUSTRALIA

Guilt free!

"Salvation is found in no one else,
for there is no other name given under heaven by which we must be saved."

ACTS 4:12

Guilt-free ice cream. Guilt-free vacations. Guilt-free living.
Although there is no such thing as living life completely free of guilt, we can be redeemed, and through the grace and mercy of Jesus Christ, we can receive the gift of starting over.

In a letter written to a small community of young believers who lived in the city of Rome, the apostle Paul clearly explained that peace and direction come only through the salvation found in Jesus Christ. Paradoxically, a guilt-free life begins by admitting we are guilty. We are not holy. Therefore, we need a Savior—someone to save us from our guilt. That need was met by God himself when he sent his Son, Jesus, to die for us.

The deed is done. The gift has been purchased. There is nothing we need to do—except accept the gift! | POWER FOR LIFE BIBLE

PITTSTOWN, NEW JERSEY, USA

Happiness is a choice

*"He sent the people to their homes,
joyful and glad in heart for the good things the Lord had done."*

2 CHRONICLES 7:10

Happiness isn't a state of being...it's a state of consciousness. It's an intentional decision you and I make.

I was raised in a very positive home. In the mornings, we all had breakfast together. These breakfasts were a perfect way to send us off to conquer the world. They always included a time of devotions where we would sing a song, read the Bible, and recite a poem. One of the poems we recited together went like this:

I'm going to be happy today,
Though the skies may be cloudy or gray.
No matter what comes my way,
I'm going to be happy today.

Happiness is a choice we make and choosing happiness makes life more fun. Whether you're married or single, rich or poor, you can still be happy. It's up to you! Choose happiness today. | ROBERT A. SCHULLER

E UNOTO, LAKE MANYARA, TANZANIA

A family resemblance

"You became imitators of us and of the Lord."

I THESSALONIANS 1:6

Physically, we all resemble our parents in some way. As a child grows, the similarities often become more pronounced. A little girl has the same endearing smile as her mother. A little boy uses his hands when he talks, just like his father does. Sometimes the similarities are genetic, as in the case of a smile, but often the similarities are learned behaviors. For example, a little girl wants a toy vacuum so she can help her mommy clean, while a little boy wants a toolset so he can work alongside his daddy in his shop. Children learn by watching their parents and by copying the behaviors they see.

Likewise, when you emulate your Heavenly Father's behaviors and are merciful, gracious, compassionate, kind, patient, and loving—people can't help but notice that you are your Father's child. | ROBERT A. SCHULLER

OLD ROMAN ROAD, TURKEY

Stepping stones to success

*"Approach God's throne of grace with confidence…
and find grace to help in your time of need."*

HEBREWS 4:16

Failure isn't failure if you have learned from it. Then, failure can be a stepping stone to success. The only failure that is certain is failing to try and failing to learn and grow. A pole-vaulter only knows how high he can jump when he fails to get over the bar. And once that happens then and only then does he have his new goal—his stepping stone to success.

How, then, can you be afraid of failure?

Think big! Dream bold dreams! Set a goal that is so big it can only be accomplished with God's help. Then, break it down into manageable mini goals—stepping stones that will lead to fulfillment of your dream. You will see growth. Your faith will be stretched. Others will be helped.

Take the first step toward success today—dream big! Dream bravely. Move forward without fear! | SHEILA SCHULLER COLEMAN

STATUE OF ST. PAUL, ST. PETER'S CHURCH, ROME

God's powerful presence

*"Call to me and I will answer you
and tell you great and unsearchable things you do not know."*

JEREMIAH 33:3

God's presence is within—his Holy Spirit entered when Christ became your Savior. He remains as close as the air you breathe. Breathe in God's Spirit wherever you are, whatever you're doing.

Stuck in a long line at the grocery store? Breathe in God's patience.

Frustrated with a family member? Breathe in God's understanding.

Disappointed in a coworker? Breathe in God's grace.

Facing financial obstacles? Breathe in God's provision.

Burdened with health concerns? Breathe in God's miracle healing.

No burden is too small to bring to God. No person too insignificant for his love. Nothing thrills God more than your prayers...inhaled whenever, wherever. Nothing heals more than the powerful presence of God. Tap into his presence today! | SHEILA SCHULLER COLEMAN

MONA VALE ROCK POOL, NEW SOUTH WALES, AUSTRALIA

Right person, right time

"For whoever is not against you is for you."

LUKE 9:50

One of our first members was Rosie Gray, who had become infirm following a stroke. God used Rosie, who could only attend drive-in services, to guide us to build the church he wanted—a church where people could either sit inside or in their cars.

And God provided Rosie's husband Warren—the right man at just the right time—to achieve his purposes! When we were short three thousand dollars, just hours before escrow was to close on the land, Warren said, "I can do more. Rosie needs that church. And after Rosie is gone, others will need it. Meet me at the bank."

An hour later, the exact amount needed was delivered, with just one hour to spare.

God will provide the right person you need. Ask him to send the right person, and then be willing to accept the help! | POWER FOR LIFE BIBLE

GERRINGONG, NEW SOUTH WALES, AUSTRALIA

Got milk?

*"Crave pure spiritual milk,
so that by it you may grow up in your salvation."*

I PETER 2:2

I grew up thinking that if you drank enough milk, there wasn't anything you couldn't do. And I was probably one of the top milk drinkers in the country. I didn't drink it by the pint, quart, or even the gallon. I drank it by the barrel!

Unfortunately, I developed a horrible case of cystic acne over my entire body. It was very painful, and nothing I did to get rid of it worked.

One day while getting a haircut, my barber said, "Robert, I bet if you stopped drinking milk, you would solve your problem."

Quit drinking milk? After finding no other solution, I finally quit drinking milk. And guess what? The acne went away in a matter of weeks.

Sometimes the "knowledge" we acquire is bad. But to grow big and strong spiritually, we need the milk of God's word. | ROBERT A. SCHULLER

SUNRISE, PYRAMIDS AT GIZA, EGYPT

Hold on. Hope in God.

"Guide me in your truth and teach me, for you are God my Savior, and my hope is in you all day long."

PSALM 25:5

When tough times come, hold on...expectantly...trusting God. Trust God's positive plan for your life. That doesn't mean an absence of obstacles. It means belief that God can use anything and everything in your life to accomplish his perfect will.

Can you remember when you thought you were following God's plan then reached the end of your rope? You saw nothing good coming from it. Maybe you earned an academic degree you now will never use. Maybe a business you started ended up in bankruptcy.

Can God use even *that*? Don't be surprised when you look back at twists and turns, apparent false-starts, even "failures" to discover that all of it was part of God's plan—his plan for good, to give you a future and a hope!

Hold on. Pray expectantly. Hope and believe that God will never, ever let you down! | SHEILA SCHULLER COLEMAN

JENNE FARM, WOODSTOCK, VERMONT, USA

Your dream is God's gift to you.

ROBERT H. SCHULLER

September

THE REMARKABLES, SOUTH AUSTRALIA, AUSTRALIA

God's masterpiece

"For we are God's handiwork, created in Christ Jesus to do good works, which God prepared in advance for us to do."

EPHESIANS 2:10

Many people, like water, follow the path of least resistance when it comes to pursuing God's vision, dream, and purpose for their life and they ultimately end up in the same place water ends up—at the lowest spot possible.

Because you are "God's masterpiece," you are uniquely designed and specifically gifted to "do the good things God planned for you long ago (Ephesians 2:10; Psalm 139:14-16). If you want to fulfill your God-given dream, then you'll have to take the high road, climb the mountains, and allow God to work in you and through you.

How do you discover your "God-designed" mission? It begins with prayer continues with Bible study, and moves into community with positive people who believe, like you do, that God will do miracles in your life to make that dream come true. | ROBERT A. SCHULLER

GOD'S MARBLES, NORTHERN TERRITORY, AUSTRALIA

Best friends forever

"He is altogether lovely...this is my friend."

SONG OF SOLOMON 5:16

BFF: Instant Messaging shorthand for Best Friends Forever. Teens throw this around carelessly, changing "best friends *forever*" from one week to the next, with as little thought as changing their hairstyle or their clothes.

Yet, who of us hasn't longed for a BFF, a best friend *forever*? Most of us have friends that last most of our lives. Many of us have a spouse who is our best friend. But there is a friend who is closer, who loves us just the way we are—foibles, idiosyncrasies, and all. He is a friend who will never leave us—for all eternity—an eternal, omnipotent BFF: Jesus Christ—Best Friend Forever!

| SHEILA SCHULLER COLEMAN

SNAKE RIVER, GRAND TETON NATIONAL PARK, WYOMING, USA

A compelling purpose

"For to me, to live is Christ..."

PHILIPPIANS 1:21

His caricature is as famous as his name. His customary "Thanks for the memories" underscored his enthusiasm for life.

What made Bob Hope such a legendary entertainer? Was it that his joy and laughter brought relief to the weary? Was it the hope he found and shared through humor? Or was it his selfless service in bringing Christmas wishes to American troops stationed in war zones throughout the world? It was all these things—and more. He was a perennially optimistic man on a lifelong mission.

Bob Hope was unselfishly driven to bring healthy humor into the world. He always had time for charity events. He taught millions of people, including his own children, about the gift of giving.

There must be a compelling purpose and mission in your life. We all need to know that we can and will make a difference. | ROBERT H. SCHULLER

YARRA RIVER, VICTORIA, AUSTRALIA

Synchronize

"Oh, that my ways were steadfast in obeying your decrees!"

PSALM 119:5

Millard Fuller was a lawyer, businessman and millionaire when his wife left him. The Fullers felt their wealthy lifestyle had driven them away from God and apart from each other. To save their marriage, the Fullers decided to take a big step—"to give all their stuff away."

Not only did that decision save their marriage, but Habitat for Humanity was born. Millard's personal mission is to eliminate poverty housing. He bases his mission on one of the most important values in Scripture: "Love your neighbor as yourself."

Millard Fuller learned to synchronize his values with his vision and holds to these unwavering moral truths: The end does *not* justify the means. God's word is the absolute moral compass for life. And loving God and others must drive every decision we make as it concerns our goals and dreams.

ROBERT A. SCHULLER

SUNSET AT NIMROD FORTRESS, ISRAEL

The power of yes

"As soon as Jesus was baptized...heaven was opened...and a voice from heaven said, 'This is my Son, whom I love; with him I am well pleased.'"

MATTHEW 3:16-17

Crystal Cathedral Ministries will never forget the day when Evel Knievel, the renowned motorcycle stunt man, asked to be baptized. As the world watched him repent and proclaim his faith in Jesus Christ as his Lord and Savior, Dr. Robert H. Schuller baptized him. Tears streaming down his face, Evel was a new creation.

Since that day, thousands more have been baptized, giving their lives to Jesus Christ, cleansing their souls, making a public profession of their faith.

If God can use someone like Evel Knievel to spark an awakening at the Crystal Cathedral, if God can use a scruffy fellow such as John the Baptist to introduce Jesus to the world, God can certainly use you, too, to make a difference. All it takes is being willing to say yes! | POWER FOR LIFE BIBLE

SOUTH SKILLION SUNRISE, TERRIGAL, NEW SOUTH WALES, AUSTRALIA

Ask boldly

"Take delight in the Lord
and he will give you the desires of your heart."

PSALM 37:4

What do you want but are afraid to ask for? More faith? Better health? Financial security? More time? The love of your life?

It is never too late to ask. You deserve the best. You have the right to ask. In fact, Jesus Christ urges you to ask for what you want: "You have not because you ask not."

So, ask away. Approach God boldly and tell him your heart's desire. If you have committed your way to him and your will is aligned with his, then chances are your desires are his desires. He infuses all of his children with his desires as a way of achieving his purposes. Trust the desires he has given you and ask him to either fulfill the desire or remove it. Then open your spiritual eyes and see God at work granting you your heart's desire!

SHEILA SCHULLER COLEMAN

WATERWELL, BANGLADESH

Employers and employees

"Masters, provide your [employees] with what is right and fair, because you know that you also have a Master in heaven."

COLOSSIANS 4:1

A faithful employer is one you can count on to pay an honest day's wage for an honest day's work.

Dennis Washington understood this principle. At the age of twenty-nine, he borrowed $30,000 and went into business for himself and was quite successful. But his big break came when he bought the Anaconda Copper Mine in Butte, Montana.

The mine workers there had been on strike for three years. Washington knew there was plenty of ore and that if he could just create peace with the unions, everyone could go back to work. So he proposed that the workers accept lower salaries in return for a share of the mine's profits. The employees accepted Washington's proposal. Five years later they were the highest paid mine workers in the world.

Mutual fairness and loyalty are the foundation of a moral work ethic.

| ROBERT A. SCHULLER

TRADITIONAL FOOD OF JESUS' DAY, ISRAEL

Work smart, then hard

"It is appropriate for people to eat, to drink and to find satisfaction in their toilsome labor...during the few days of life God has given them."

ECCLESIASTES 5:18

I have a friend who painted houses his whole life. He charged twenty dollars an hour for his labor and because he was self-employed, had no benefits. Everything he needed, he provided for himself. He lived in a comfortable home and put money away for a "rainy day" and retirement... which came about the same time, and sooner than expected, due to a stroke. So he had to stop work and rely on the proceeds from his own hard and smart work through the years.

Today, he's sitting pretty. For thirty-five years he put ten percent of his income into savings and took advantage of the "eighth wonder of the world"—the power of compounding interest.

It's impossible to outsmart life. But if you work, save, and plan for the future, it's reasonable to expect your future needs will be taken care of.

ROBERT A. SCHULLER

PETUNIAS, RIPLEY CASTLE, YORKSHIRE, UK

The be-happy attitudes

"I have learned the secret of being content in any and every situation, whether well fed or hungry, whether living in plenty or in want."

PHILIPPIANS 4:12

Happiness! Elusive, isn't it?

How often have you thought: "If only I had that car...then I'd be satisfied!"

"If only I could find someone who truly loves me...then I'd be happy!"

"If only I wasn't under so much financial pressure...then I'd be content!"

Truth is, all of the "if onlys" in the world—*even if they all came true*—still don't guarantee us happiness. Neither do fame, fortune, recognition, or relationships.

So, where *do* we find happiness?

God's word offers us a solution in the "Beatitudes." These eight positive attitude-adjusting principles come straight from the opening lines of Jesus' famous Sermon on the Mount found in Matthew 5:5-10. And for over two thousand years their timeless truths have transformed the minds, moods, and manners of men and women worldwide.

Discover them! Apply them! And find happiness in living them!

| ROBERT H. SCHULLER

NATURAL ARCH, QUEENSLAND, AUSTRALIA

The poor in spirit

"Blessed are the poor in spirit,
for theirs is the kingdom of heaven."

MATTHEW 5:3

Poverty isn't just a matter of finances! All of us face some kind of poverty; every one of us has a need at some level in our lives. Maybe it's *financial* poverty. Or it might be *occupational* poverty: we either lack success in our chosen profession or merely lack direction, a dream, or goals. It could also be *intellectual* or *emotional* poverty.

Jesus begins the Beatitudes with a tremendous principle that has to do with the question of poverty: *"Blessed are the poor in spirit, for theirs is the kingdom of heaven."* The secret of successful living is simple: Discover your soft spot, your weak link, your ignorant area, your poverty pocket. Then become "poor in spirit"—face up to your poverty, humble yourself before God, acknowledge your weakness, and ask for help.

Blessings promise to follow. | ROBERT H. SCHULLER

MOSAIC OF LAZARUS COMING OUT OF THE TOMB, CHURCH OF SAINT LAZARUS, HOLY LAND

The comforted

"Blessed are those who mourn, for they will be comforted."

MATTHEW 5:4

People often ask me, "Dr. Schuller, why do bad things happen to good people?" Perhaps the better question is: "What happens to good people when bad things happen to them?"

As a pastor, I am often in the position of dealing with hurt, lonely, suffering, sick, and dying people. I've trudged across lush green cemetery lawns with my arms around young wives, husbands, fathers, mothers, and family members. I have watched hundreds of caskets lowered into the ground wrapped in flowers and flags. I've seen people buried in graduation gowns, pulpit attire, and bridal dresses. And over and over as I've watched people in their grief, I've witnessed this: *God comforts good people when bad things happen to them.*

Trouble never leaves us where it finds us. God comes and comforts so when bad things happen to good people...they become better people!

| ROBERT H. SCHULLER

JESUS WITH MARY AND MARTHA, CHURCH OF SAINT LAZARUS, HOLY LAND

The mighty

"Blessed are the meek, for they will inherit the earth."

MATTHEW 5:5

Who's stronger—the young man who gives in to his rage and becomes physically or verbally abusive? Or the young man who remains calm, assured of his inner strength?

The powerful are mighty when they learn to restrain their power. They know that real might lies in control and discipline. The mighty remain gentle while building strength. They are merciful when exercising might. The mighty do not merely win a war; they win the hearts of a nation! And they are blessed.

The weak are also mighty when they turn their problems into projects, their sorrows into servants, their obstacles into opportunities, their tragedies into triumphs, their stumbling blocks into stepping stones. They see interruptions as interesting interludes. They harvest fruit from frustration. They convert enemies into friends. They look upon adversities as adventures.

Who are the mighty? The meek. | ROBERT H. SCHULLER

ATLANTIS FALLS, WESTERN AUSTRALIA, AUSTRALIA

The righteous

"Blessed are those who hunger and thirst for righteousness,
for they will be filled."

MATTHEW 5:6

Satisfaction, happiness, fulfillment...these are as elusive and fleeting as shadows when we look for them in fame, success, power, sex, or money. Jesus said, "Blessed are those who hunger and thirst for *righteousness*, for they shall be *filled*." Here he's telling us that we can satisfy our heart's deepest hunger, its deepest longing, by seeking righteousness.

Righteousness isn't merely successfully avoiding temptation. Nor is it absolute holiness or about living perfect lives. We all make mistakes. We all commit sin.

The psalmist says that the *righteous* "are like a tree planted by streams of water, which yields its fruit in season and whose leaf does not wither— whatever they do prospers" (Psalm 1:3).

Satisfaction comes in knowing we are worthwhile, valuable persons who are making a difference—that our lives count for something GREAT!

| ROBERT H. SCHULLER

LIFFEY FALLS, TASMANIA, AUSTRALIA

The merciful

"Blessed are the merciful,
for they will be shown mercy."

MATTHEW 5:7

If you want to change your world, change yourself.

How do you do that? I know of only one way. It happens when you meet Jesus Christ and ask him to take over your life. Only Christ can take a heart that's been filled with fear, anger, bitterness, and hurt and liberate it with his mercy.

But to treat people mercifully, you first have to learn to treat yourself with mercy. Accept yourself as Christ accepts you—just as you are! If you lack a deep inner sense of self-worth, you will constantly have problems with other people. You will be unkind, critical, and a gossip. You'll lash back. And eventually you will undermine the most important aspects of your life and it will collapse all around you.

Follow Christ's example. Be merciful and God will step in and show you mercy, too. | ROBERT H. SCHULLER

NORTH SHORE, OAHU, HAWAII, USA

The pure in heart

"Blessed are the pure in heart, for they will see God."

MATTHEW 5:8

Some boys were watching Leonardo da Vinci paint when one of them knocked over a stack of canvases. The artist threw down his brush and hurled harsh words at the lad, who ran from the studio crying.

Da Vinci picked up his brush to begin working again, but couldn't. (He'd been trying to paint the face of Jesus.)

The artist put down his brush, went to the streets, and searched until he found the boy he had scolded. "I'm sorry, son," he said, "I shouldn't have spoken to you so harshly. Please forgive me. You only knocked over the canvases. I blocked the flow of God in my life with my anger." Da Vinci returned to his painting. This time Jesus' face flowed freely from his brush.

Negative emotions block our relationship with God. Deal with them. That's what the "pure in heart" do. | ROBERT H. SCHULLER

WATENDLATH, LAKES DISTRICT, UK

Peacemakers

"Blessed are the peacemakers, for they will be called children of God."

MATTHEW 5:9

How do you want to be remembered? What kind of reputation do you crave? Jesus is saying in the seventh beatitude that happiness comes from caring about your reputation for the right reason. What's that? To be known as "children of God."

And how do you build a reputation as a beautiful child of God? By being a peacemaker. Isaiah 58:12 says, "...be called Repairer of Broken Walls, Restorer of Streets with Dwellings."

We see breaches all around us. We see them in families, between labor and management, between nations, and between political parties. Being a peacemaker is risky. But it's essential if breaches are to be repaired.

When God sees a breach, he builds a bridge. And he calls us to do the same by being peacemakers. Be a peacemaker and your reputation as a child of God will shine. | ROBERT H. SCHULLER

SNOWY RIVER COUNTRY, VICTORIA, AUSTRALIA

The persecuted

*"Blessed are those who are persecuted because of righteousness,
for theirs is the kingdom of heaven."*

MATTHEW 5:10

The final lesson Jesus taught in the Beatitudes is perhaps the toughest one to learn.

If, after applying all of the prior principles to your experience, you still find yourself being persecuted—you must choose to believe that God will settle the score in his time and in his way.

Persecution wears many faces! For some, persecution takes the form of physical torture. Persecution also wears the face of harassment, snubs, rejection, and discrimination. It occurs at various times and strikes from a variety of sources. At times, we may even persecute ourselves with regrets, guilt, and remorse!

So how can you be happy when facing persecution? Here are seven suggestions: Stay positive, be prepared, persevere in doing what's right, pardon those who hurt you, persist in trusting God, pray for understanding and strength, and remember...this too shall pass. | ROBERT H. SCHULLER

THE LABYRINTH, TASMANIA, AUSTRALIA

Dream power

"But the plans of the Lord stand firm forever,
the purposes of his heart through all generations."

PSALM 33:11

Joseph was a dreamer. As a boy his dreams often made those around him jealous—especially his brothers. But when God led Joseph from the sheep pastures in Canaan to the palaces of Pharaoh in Egypt, God used Joseph's ability to interpret dreams to save his family and the nation of Israel from famine.

God had a plan for Joseph—one that took him through some rough days. But God used every setback Joseph experienced for his ultimate good and God's perfect purposes.

Have you ever gotten discouraged because of obstacles you've faced waiting for God's plans for you to come true? Obstacles like financial setbacks or unforeseen changes in your plans? Every obstacle is an opportunity for God to achieve his purposes.

Ask God to make his plans clear, and then give it everything you've got to make it a reality. | POWER FOR LIFE BIBLE

BRISBANE WATER, NEW SOUTH WALES, AUSTRALIA

Say yes to the dream!

"The Lord said, 'Whom shall I send? And who will go for us?'
And I said, 'Here am I. Send me!'"

ISAIAH 6:8

W hat would you do if you knew you could not fail?" How often has Dr. Robert H. Schuller challenged us with those words? Yet how many even dare to give voice to such dreams? It is not your lack of skills, or education, or knowledge that holds you back from reaching your full potential. It's your lack of faith, your inability to believe in yourself and in God.

Imagine standing before God at the end of your life and being shown all that you could have done had you just had more faith! God's work needs people just like you who are courageous enough to dream big. The bigger your dream, the more you can do for others. Think of all the people you can help just by saying yes to God's dream for your life. Say "Yes" to God today.

| SHEILA SCHULLER COLEMAN

CARDO MAXIMUS, JERASH, JORDAN

Care, commit, conquer!

"Give careful thought to the paths for your feet and be steadfast in all your ways."

PROVERBS 4:26

When you are building your God-given dream, working on the plan God has for your life, there will be times when you may have to rebuild. There may be times when you will face ridicule and even threatening opposition.

The secret to getting through those tough times, the secret to rebuilding, is *care* and *commitment*. If you don't care, you won't have the desire, the motivation to carry you through the dark days. If you don't have the commitment, you will give up when you face opposition, and it will never get built.

God needs builders and, at times, rebuilders. He will never ask you to build or rebuild on your own. He will always provide the assistance and encouragement you need. However, he does need you to care and commit to seeing it done. | POWER FOR LIFE BIBLE

PUFFING BILLY, DANDENONGS, VICTORIA, AUSTRALIA

Success through failure

*"They tried to enter Bithynia,
but the Spirit of Jesus would not allow them to."*

ACTS 16:7

I dreamed of being a pediatrician. Although I did well in my studies, I didn't have the 4.0 needed to get into medical school. All applications to medical schools brought rejection letters, so I knew God had closed that door.

Years later, after our four boys were grown, God called me into education. I earned two credentials and a Masters degree. Then one day a University of California, Irvine, pamphlet came across my desk. Finally, God was opening a door for me to become a doctor!

I have now completed my Ed.D. program and am using it writing Sunday school curriculum. God's call, years earlier, was not to pediatrics, saving children's lives physically. Instead his call was to save children's lives spiritually.

I thank God daily for allowing my apparent failure so I could find and succeed at his call for my life! | SHEILA SCHULLER COLEMAN

COSSACK, WESTERN AUSTRALIA, AUSTRALIA

Pursue or pull back?

"Discretion will protect you,
and understanding will guard you."

PROVERBS 2:11

There are times when it is important to push full-steam ahead, regardless of the obstacles. And then there are times when it is more prudent to back down.

Ironically, it frequently takes a bigger person to back down, and it always takes a wise person to know which action is the most appropriate. Was Christ weak for going to the cross without a fight? Of course not! Does turning the other cheek mean you are weak? Never! You can discern a course of action by asking yourself the following questions: "What will I lose if I change my course, and what will I lose if I don't?" "What will I gain if I change my course, and what will I gain if I don't?"

There are times when the wise, prudent course of action is to change your course. | POWER FOR LIFE BIBLE

PEARLING LUGGER, BROOME, WESTERN AUSTRALIA, AUSTRALIA

Called to courage

"They saw the courage of Peter and John...
realized that they were ordinary men...and that they had been with Jesus."

ACTS 4:13

Courage is what you need when you recognize the inherent danger in a bold goal, when you're hesitant to step into a situation rife with the possibility of embarrassment, when you won't risk making a mistake, even though it might help others in the process. Taking a stand, jumping in to save a life, daring to dream a noble dream, being brave enough to declare a big, hairy, audacious goal requires courage!

Find courage in its converse. Be afraid—to fail to live up to your potential. Be afraid—to neglect to help. Be afraid—to reach the end of your life only to discover all you could have done, but didn't.

If you are more afraid of failing to act than you are afraid of failing, then you will find the courage you need to be all that God needs you to be!

| SHEILA SCHULLER COLEMAN

CAMELS, CABLE BEACH, BROOME, WESTERN AUSTRALIA, AUSTRALIA

A minority of one

*"There is a future hope for you,
and your hope will not be cut off."*

PROVERBS 24:14

Have you ever felt like a minority of one?

A little boy in Italy at the end of the last century sure did. He believed God had called him to sing. So one day he visited a voice teacher to get an appraisal. The teacher listened, and after he was finished stated emphatically, "Your voice sounds like wind crashing through a shutter. You're the worst singer I've ever heard."

Not to be detoured, the boy looked for any opportunity to learn to sing. He sang Neapolitan folk songs on the street and at age nine, joined the parish choir. It wasn't until he was a teenager that he took his first voice lesson. Who was this boy with the big desire to sing? Enrico Caruso, one of the world's greatest tenors.

Never let others' opinions keep you from pursuing your God-given dreams.

ROBERT A. SCHULLER

BATTLEBORO COMMON, VERMONT, USA

For goodness' sake

*"There is a time for everything,
and a season for every activity under heaven."*

ECCLESIASTES 3:1

Goodness isn't always kind.

Consider the mother eagle. She builds her nest in the top of a tall tree or on a mountain cliff where she lays her eggs and tenderly watches over them until they hatch. Then she pours a great deal of time and energy into caring for her young. She feeds them, keeps them warm, and defends them against every danger.

Finally it's time for the eaglets to leave the nest. What does mama eagle do? She kicks her eaglets out of the nest! Mother eagle knows that for her young to soar among the clouds, they have to leave "home"...and she provides the impetus!

There *is* a time for kindness in life. But there's also a time for goodness. Goodness draws a line; it sets boundaries. Is it time to exercise a little "goodness" in your life? | ROBERT A. SCHULLER

FERN GULLY, VICTORIA, AUSTRALIA

Generosity begins with ten percent

"'Bring the whole tithe...test me in this,' says the Lord Almighty,
'and see if I will not throw open the floodgates of heaven and pour out
so much blessing that there will not be room enough to store it.'"

MALACHI 3:10

I worked my way through college as a janitor at a women's club. I did some of the dirtiest work imaginable. When I got my paycheck, I gave ten percent back to God. That was hard for me to do because I had so little. My parents were barely surviving. Our farm had just been blown away by a tornado. We had lost everything. And I was trying to stay in school in the midst of that financial disaster.

It was tempting to rationalize and tell God I needed the money more than he did—that I would wait and tithe when things got better. But I didn't wait. I gave the Lord the first tenth of what I earned—a practice I follow to this day. God wants us to trust him with our money. When we do, he blesses us.

ROBERT H. SCHULLER

ROAD TO MT. WEDGE, NORTHERN TERRITORY, AUSTRALIA

Conflicted? Confused?

"The crooked roads shall become straight,
the rough ways smooth."

LUKE 3:5

Life's maze can be overwhelming. Which way do you turn? What do you believe? Who do you trust? Conflicting advice makes finding your way even more confusing. You are unable to see the big picture. All you can see are the barriers, fences, and hedges. Imagine having a lookout tower where you could see the entire maze and gain direction from above. What comfort that would be!

God's "bird's-eye view" solves your dilemma. If you connect with God, you will have all the guidance you need. He may not tell you, "turn left" or "take this fork." He provides guidance through his Word, through opportunities, prayer, and positive ideas. You don't need the bird's-eye view. You won't be stumped by towering barriers with the omnipotent, omniscient God of the universe guiding you. Connect with him. Simply pray, "Show me the way."

| SHEILA SCHULLER COLEMAN

GRAPE VINES, MOUNT OLYMPUS, GREECE

Be amazed

"What Jesus did here in Cana of Galilee was the first of the signs through which he revealed his glory; and his disciples put their faith in him."

JOHN 2:11

It takes many years to make a fine wine. It is a complex, artistic, and scientific endeavor. During Jesus' time, winemaking was an important undertaking, for water was not safe to drink but wine was.

Jesus' first miracle—evidence that he was the Messiah—was turning water into wine at a wedding in Cana. This miracle teaches us not only about the miracle-working power of Christ, but also that there is no miracle too silly, too insignificant for him. He cares about all facets of our lives just as he cared about the hosts of the wedding, not wanting them to be embarrassed in front of friends and family when they ran out of this important beverage.

What miracle do you need but are afraid to ask for because it might be too petty? Ask away! Jesus loves to amaze us! | POWER FOR LIFE BIBLE

LAGOON BEACH, LORD HOWE ISLAND, NEW SOUTH WALES, AUSTRALIA

Eternal life

*"For God so loved the world that he gave his one and only Son,
that whoever believes in him shall not perish but have eternal life."*

JOHN 3:16

When I was eight years old my father took me to hear Billy Graham in the Los Angeles Coliseum. We sat in the bleachers along with everyone else. Even though I was raised in the church, knew all the Bible stories, and knew I wanted to be a preacher when I grew up, when Billy Graham gave the invitation for people to go forward and dedicate their lives to Christ, I knew he was talking to me. So I went forward that day. A counselor talked and prayed with me and I gave my life to Christ.

Jesus said, "I am the Way, the Truth, and the Life. No one comes to the Father except through me" (John 14:6). If you don't have a relationship with Jesus Christ, I urge you today to receive the gift of life God offers you.

| ROBERT A. SCHULLER

LUCKY BAY, CAPE LE GRAND NATIONAL PARK, WESTERN AUSTRALIA, AUSTRALIA

Touch the world

"Whatever you did for one of the least of these brothers and sisters of mine,
you did for me."

MATTHEW 25:40

The problems in this world can seem overwhelming. Everywhere you look, people are being affected by crime, poverty, sickness, loneliness, and grief. At times, it can feel like we're swimming in an ocean of tears. And then we turn on the evening news to hear the latest horror from Bosnia or Rwanda or wherever people have decided to slaughter and maim their neighbors and former friends. The problems in this world just seem too big to face.

God doesn't expect you and me to solve all the world's problems. He simply asks us to make a difference wherever and however we can—one person at a time. Whenever we reach out to the less fortunate—one of the people Scripture calls "the least of these"—it's like reaching out to Christ.

Touch the world—one step, one person at a time. | ROBERT A. SCHULLER

GLADE CREEK GRIST MILL, WEST VIRGINIA, USA

Peace begins with you and me.

ROBERT A. SCHULLER

October

SYDNEY HARBOUR BRIDGE, NEW SOUTH WALES, AUSTRALIA

"You are wonderful!"

"The Lord your God is with you…
he will take great delight in you."

ZEPHANIAH 3:17

A famous singer was scheduled to perform at the Paris Opera House. The auditorium was packed. The curtain went up. But the famous singer never appeared. The house manager stepped up to the microphone and said: "The man you've come to hear tonight is ill and won't be performing. Someone new is standing in for him." The manager said the stand-in's name, but no one heard it over the audience's groan of disappointment. When the unknown singer finished, there was nothing but stony silence. Suddenly, from high up in the balconies, a little boy stood up and shouted, "Daddy, I think you were wonderful!" The crowd broke into thunderous applause.

Self-esteem cannot be gained by position or performance. Your security and self-esteem most be rooted in Jesus Christ. Like that little boy, Jesus shouts to you, "I think you're wonderful!" | ROBERT H. SCHULLER

NORTH AVOCA BEACH, NEW SOUTH WALES, AUSTRALIA

The person God sees

"She gave this name to the Lord who spoke to her:
'You are the God who sees me,' for she said, 'I have now seen the One who sees me.'"

GENESIS 16:13

A beggar sat across the street from an artist's studio. From his window the portrait painter sketched the face of the defeated, despairing soul—with two important changes. In the dull eyes of the beggar he put the flashing hint of an inspired dreamer. He sketched the man's face reflecting an iron will and fierce determination. When the portrait was finished, the artist called the poor man over to see it.

"Who is it?" he asked as the artist smiled quietly. Then, catching just a glimpse of himself in this portrait, the beggar hesitantly asked, "Is it me? Can *that* possibly be me?"

"That's how I see you," replied the artist.

Straightening his shoulders, the beggar responded, "If that's the man you see—then that's the man I'll be."

God looks at you and sees a beautiful person waiting to be born!

| ROBERT H. SCHULLER

WHITEHAVEN BEACH, QUEENSLAND, AUSTRALIA

It pays to trust

"When I am afraid,
I put my trust in you."

PSALM 56:3

I once read a scientific analysis in *American Psychologist* magazine about trust and human behavior. It stated that people who trust, don't easily fall for a con, are more successful in business and their personal lives, are healthier, and often have more money.

At first glance, the report may seem shocking. And yet, it makes sense. People who don't trust are often cynical. Cynics demand proof for everything. They won't make a move unless they're certain it's the right one. They don't trust anyone whose credentials they haven't checked out thoroughly. And they don't invest in something unless they're positive they can't lose. Before long, they are no longer taking chances and their lives are filled with failure, stress, and illness.

It pays to trust. Sure, you're going to lose at times or make mistakes. But bottom line—trust is the best way to live. | ROBERT H. SCHULLER

TOTEM POLE, MONUMENT VALLEY, ARIZONA, USA

Wilderness wanderings

"Say to those with fearful hearts,
'Be strong, do not fear; your God will come...
water will gush forth in the wilderness and streams in the desert.'"

ISAIAH 35:4,6

Trudging through searing heat, parched, with no shade in sight—this can be a description of one's spiritual journey every now and then. All followers of Christ find themselves wandering in the wilderness at times. Lost. Confused. Feeling abandoned by God. Unable to see his hand at work, you feel like your faith is dying.

Are these wanderings a symptom of disobedience? Are they a form of punishment? Are they due to a lack of faithfulness? The truth is, even the most mature followers of Jesus Christ have times in their lives of spiritual drought and confusion. God allows us to wander in the wilderness because it is in the wilderness that we find and fully appreciate the streams. It is in the valleys that we are forced to grow and learn lessons that we would never learn in paradise. | SHEILA SCHULLER COLEMAN

PINE VALLEY, CRADLE MOUNTAIN, TASMANIA

Comfort in God's presence

"May he be enthroned in God's presence forever;
appoint your love and faithfulness to protect him."

PSALM 61:7

I experience God's presence in my life when I read the psalms. It's amazing how similar my life experiences and feelings are to David's. God was with David when he was feeling defeated, alone, or abandoned. He stayed close to David even when he was weak and sinful. God took David through times of defeat, loneliness, and weakness. And in the end David shouted God's praises.

So how does someone practice the presence of God in their life? Here's what I do: I spend time in prayer and meditation, and listen for God's voice. I also journal; I write down the things I pray about, keep a list of ways my prayers are answered, and record the impressions and insights that come from waiting for God to speak.

God comforts me with his presence. He can do the same for you.

| ROBERT A. SCHULLER

BURRA HOMESTEAD, SOUTH AUSTRALIA, AUSTRALIA

Brokenhearted?

*"The Lord is close to the brokenhearted
and saves those who are crushed in spirit."*

PSALM 34:18

There's nothing more painful than a broken heart. Feeling unloved, uncared for, unworthy can induce emotional and physical disease. Soul wounds prevent you from daring to trust, daring to believe, daring to love again. Unwilling to risk being hurt again, you choose the path of loneliness.

How could a loving God allow such hurt? Couldn't a powerful Lord have prevented your heartbreak? Where was he when your world tumbled down, when your dreams were all dashed?

God cares about your broken heart. It grieves him to see his children hurt each other. But he will carry you through times of hurt. He will heal your wounds, turn your scars into stars, and your hurts into halos. He can redeem brokenness and make you whole again with his care and his powerful, healing love. | SHEILA SCHULLER COLEMAN

SHEPHERDS ON THE ROAD TO EPHRAIM (TAYBA), HOLY LAND

Jesus, our Good Shepherd

*"[Jesus said,] 'I am the good shepherd.
The good shepherd lays down his life for the sheep.'"*

JOHN 10:11

Jesus frequently taught using stories. In John 10, he used comparison and contrast to explain how he guides and protects his people: A robber tries to sneak over the back wall. A shepherd enters by way of the door. The sheep know the shepherd's voice. They don't know the voice of a robber. He explained, "I am the good shepherd. I know my sheep, and my sheep know me" (John 10:14).

How reassuring to know that Jesus would willingly lay down his life to protect us from harm and dangers that threaten to rob us of our joy and lives. He seeks to protect us from distractions, fears, self-doubts, and destructive pleasures that keep us from making a positive difference with our lives.

Do you need the Good Shepherd in your life? Invite him in—he's only a prayer away. | POWER FOR LIFE BIBLE

METAPO CRAFT CENTRE, ZIMBABWE

Life span of hurts

"He heals the brokenhearted and binds up their wounds."

PSALM 147:3

Each hurt has a different life span.

Divorce has a long life span, especially when children are involved.

Death has a long life span, too. Dr. Joyce Brothers told me after her husband Milt passed away that she grieved for over a year after his death. Many well-meaning friends tried to hurry her through her grief process, encouraging her to "get over him." Day by day, little by little, life got better. She ran on auto pilot to make it through the day. Then one day, she found herself smiling again.

Yes, hurts have different life spans. The point I want to make is this: The pain you are feeling today, whatever your hurt, will pass in time. It will likely leave a scar. But you will get through it. Trust God and your own healing process...you *will* smile again...I promise. | ROBERT H. SCHULLER

CAPE NEDDICK LIGHTHOUSE, MAINE, USA

Obstacle or opportunity?

"Do not be anxious about anything, but in every situation,
by prayer and petition, with thanksgiving, present your requests to God."

PHILIPPIANS 4:6

Bumps in the road.

Obstacles in the board room.

Lack of funding.

Loss of energy.

Disappointments in treasured relationships.

The positive anticipation that fueled the beginning of the endeavor has been replaced with the painful reality of running smack dab into hard times Now what? Now is when you dig in your heels. You ask for help with an open mind, but you don't give up! You replay the reason why you wanted to start this in the first place. Was it God's noble dream? Then, trust God's sovereignty and his timing. Thank him that he will supply grace to view this obstacle as his opportunity for you to grow, to learn, to be stronger than ever. Trust God to redirect, if necessary, to see his perfect plan become a positive reality.

| SHEILA SCHULLER COLEMAN

PEMAQUID POINT LIGHTHOUSE, MAINE, USA

Heart-to-heart talks

"Pour out your heart to him,
for God is your refuge."

PSALM 62:8

My kids are into "Instant Messaging." I don't really understand how it works. All I know is that they can be talking online to multiple people all at the same time. Screens pop up one after another as the kids communicate via the technological wonder of IM.

There's another kind of communication that *I* much prefer. It happens when people open up and listen to each other's dreams, or hurts and pain. I call this *heart* language. Chances are, I have more heart conversations than most because I'm a pastor.

God longs to hear heart language. He waits for you to pour out your heart to him, to openly express your dreams and goals, and to trust him with your deepest needs and desires.

Turn off the IM—take time for a heart-to-heart talk with God.

ROBERT A. SCHULLER

THREE TABLE BEACH, OAHU, HAWAII, USA

Life's dark valleys

"Even though I walk through the darkest valley,
I will fear no evil, for you are with me;
your rod and your staff, they comfort me."

PSALM 23:4

The psalmist David, who was king of Israel, knew his share of bad times. His infant son died. His children's lives were a mess. One of his sons raped one of his daughters, after which another son murdered the boy who raped his sister. And then that son tried to take the kingdom away from him, forcing David and his supporters to flee for their lives.

There were few times in David's life when some sort of sinister intrigue wasn't swirling about him. And yet, through everything, David knew that the Lord was there for him. He knew he could trust God to deliver him from his enemies. He knew God was in control, and that everything would ultimately work out just the way it was supposed to.

Do you sometimes feel like God has forgotten about you? He hasn't!

| ROBERT A. SCHULLER

JOHANNA, VICTORIA, AUSTRALIA

God comforts us

"The Father of compassion and the God of all comfort…
comforts us in all our troubles, so that we can comfort those
with the comfort we ourselves receive from God."

2 CORINTHIANS 1:3-4

When our daughter, Carol, lost her leg in a motorcycle accident, my wife and I fell all over ourselves trying to comfort her. We never left Carol's side; one of us was with her constantly.

Then one day our friend, Dorothy DeBolt, the mother of fourteen adopted children all who have some type of handicap, called us. Dorothy expressed her love and concern, but also warned us that there was a right way and a wrong way to help Carol. She said, "Be careful how you comfort Carol."

How wise those words were. Carol needed comfort, not pity. Not the kind of comfort that came from drying her tears, but from lifting her attention beyond her present pain to future victories.

God comforts us. He picks us up, dries our tears, soothes our fears, and lifts our thoughts beyond the hurt. | ROBERT H. SCHULLER

SEDONA, ARIZONA, USA

Your strong protector

"The Lord is my shepherd, I lack nothing."

PSALM 23:1

As a shepherd boy, David cared for sheep, which are very dependent upon their human caretakers—their shepherds—for their protection and their lives.

Like sheep, we are totally dependent upon God to provide our spiritual protection and nourishment. Like sheep, we would be spiritually lost and even devoured without God to protect and guide us. Like sheep, we do not need to fear or worry. We can trust the Lord, our Good Shepherd, completely. All we have to do is relax, enjoy the beauty of being taken care of, and know that we will lack nothing if we trust our lives to the Lord.

Are you anxious? Fearful? Do you need spiritual protection from emotional predators? Then entrust your life to the Good Shepherd. He will stand between you and your troubles. He is your strong protector.

| POWER FOR LIFE BIBLE

CRAIG'S HUT, ALPINE NATIONAL PARK, VICTORIA, AUSTRALIA

Boundless boundaries

"Very truly I tell you, I am the gate for the sheep."

JOHN 10:7

There was a famous study of children which noted that children who played on playgrounds without fences were more likely to gather in the center of the yard. Yet children surrounded by a fence utilized every inch of space. The researcher theorized that the security of the fence gave the children the freedom to play free of fear or worry, whereas the lack of a fence, paradoxically, kept them captive to fear of the dangers that might lurk on the peripheries.

The Lord, our Good Shepherd, has a sheepfold where we can rest from stress and fear. We can take advantage of the sheepfold and feel the security within, or we can choose the open fields without any security measures. The good news is that the sheepfold is there for you—a safe place where you can go and seek refuge. | POWER FOR LIFE BIBLE

WATERFALL, MT. WHITNEY, CALIFORNIA, USA

Soul restoration

"He refreshes my soul."

PSALM 23:3

oul restoration is similar to restoring a house. You have to begin by fixing up the broken places. Then you have to maintain the house once it's all fixed up. Healing your soul is an ongoing process. And it is much easier to maintain it daily than it is to have to fix it over and over again.

Perhaps this is why David, who had firsthand experience of a troubled soul, wrote, "He guides me along the right paths for his name's sake." The Lord, our Good Shepherd, guides us *from* things that can hurt our souls and *to* things that will bring us joy and fulfillment. If we follow him, our souls will be protected.

God restores your soul by saving you, by forgiving you. He will never give up on you. You are his precious child, his precious lamb.

| POWER FOR LIFE BIBLE

GRAND CANYON, ARIZONA, USA

Light in the valley

"Even though I walk through the darkest valley,
I will fear no evil, for you are with me."

PSALM 23:4

Most of us probably grew up hearing this part of Psalm 23 as walking "through the valley of the shadow of death" (KJV). Most people—even Christians—are afraid of death (not where they are going, but going through the process). Death is inevitable. But as scary as death is, this psalm is a source of comfort.

Jesus bore the brunt of death for us. We would have had to face certain death and eternal separation from God, but Jesus died in our place to save us from this dire fate. The result is that when we die physically, we will be born into eternal life. For Christians, physical death is a spiritual homecoming. It is not the end; it is the beginning. Praise God for this unspeakable gift!

POWER FOR LIFE BIBLE

SHEPHERD, PISIDIAN ANTIOCH, TURKEY

Once lost, now found!

"Your rod and your staff, they comfort me."

PSALM 23:4

The Good Shepherd will go to all lengths to save a lost sheep. He will even leave the flock. So even though you might have strayed far from the path, even though you might be terribly lost and confused, Jesus the Good Shepherd, loves you. He searches high and low for you, using his rod to protect you, to beat the bushes and fight off predators, until he finds you. Then, using his staff, he gently pulls you up out of the dangerous ravine. Picking you up in his arms, he doesn't say, "Oh, you bad sheep! I am so disappointed in you." No, he says, "I am so glad to have you back in my arms. I love you. Welcome home!"

Then he carries you back to the fold, rejoicing that his lamb who was once lost is now found! | POWER FOR LIFE BIBLE

GALLIPOLI, TURKEY

Fights into feasts

"You prepare a table before me in the presence of my enemies."

PSALM 23:5

Peace—whether political or personal—is a priceless commodity these days and increasingly difficult to achieve. Conflict seems to be a part of everybody's lives whether at work, in the neighborhood, or even in the family. Today, the conflict you face may not be dramatic, but it is destructive nonetheless.

It is essential we learn the secret of building bridges, finding commonalities, and being peacemakers, especially in our families. Too few families are breaking bread together anymore. Too many families, if they are eating at home together at all, are eating in front of the television. The result is a breakdown in communication, which is the predecessor of all conflict. This psalm encourages us to entreat the Lord to bring peace to our lives—to turn our battles into brotherhood, our conflicts into constructive cooperation, our fights into feasts! | POWER FOR LIFE BIBLE

GRASS TREE, FLINDERS RANGES, SOUTH AUSTRALIA, AUSTRALIA

Anointed for action

"You anoint my head with oil."

PSALM 23:5

Think of when you have gone to the store to buy a gift for someone. You might have perused several stores until you found what you liked. You chose that item over every other item in all the other stores. In much the same way God chose you, then he anointed you. You bear his spiritual branding. You belong to him, and he will not let anyone take you from him. He will go to all lengths to keep you from being stolen or broken.

He did not choose you, however, just to sit on a shelf. He chose you to be a leader, to make a positive difference in your world. How can you do this? Pray and ask God to specifically guide you to where he needs you the most. Take a step today. There is no time to waste. | POWER FOR LIFE BIBLE

CAIRNS, QUEENSLAND, AUSTRALIA

Giving in gratitude

"My cup overflows."

PSALM 23:5

Hunger is a big problem in our world. One billion people suffer from hunger. Almost one in five children in America goes to bed at night hungry.

If it is true that our cups are overflowing and we have more than enough, how can we help? How can we make a tiny difference in bridging the gap between those who have more than enough and those who are lacking bare essentials? There are multiple ways that people have adopted to address this inequity. Some have chosen political paths. Others have chosen to get involved in charitable organizations, and others are quietly making a difference every day. However you feel God has called you to make a difference, be a part of those who are showing their gratitude to God for his abundance by helping those less fortunate. | POWER FOR LIFE BIBLE

FIJIAN ISLANDS, FIJI

Goodness and love

"Surely your goodness and love will follow me all the days of my life."

PSALM 23:6

What a promise this verse is—that we will be loved and forgiven every day of our lives. When we mess up, what can we do? We can go to the Good Shepherd, Jesus, whose goodness and love is limitless.

As humans, we are vastly different. For us, to forgive even once is so hard, let alone to forgive a repeated behavior. Why? Usually it is because we are afraid that forgiveness will be equated with approval, and the one we are forgiving will not learn from his or her mistake.

Yet God is less concerned with teaching us lessons. He is more interested in forgiving us, so we can be in fellowship with him once more. The love of God comes with only one string attached—that we return his love and in turn extend his love to others. | POWER FOR LIFE BIBLE

FIJIAN ISLANDS, FIJI

Heaven on earth

"And I will dwell in the house of the Lord forever."

PSALM 23:6

Some theologians have defined sin as anything that interferes with our relationship with God. Think of it as a phone line. As long as we have a strong signal, we can be in fellowship with God. But when we drive out of satellite range or a rat chews the line, the connection is lost. That is what sin can do. Sin results in our feeling guilty, and then we are afraid to look God in the face. When that happens, we are not experiencing God's presence; we are not experiencing the joys of heaven here on earth.

But when we repent of and confess our shortcomings, our sins, to God, and accept his grace and mercy, we can reconnect with him. We don't have to wait to know how wonderful heaven will be, because we can experience glimpses of it here today. | POWER FOR LIFE BIBLE

ARKABA WOOLSHED, FLINDERS RANGES, SOUTH AUSTRALIA, AUSTRALIA

Tough faith for tough times

*"Whatever you have learned or received or heard from me,
or seen in me—put it into practice. And the God of peace will be with you."*

PHILIPPIANS 4:9

The dreaded call about Dad undergoing brain surgery in Amsterdam came in the middle of the night. Prognosis uncertain, Mom and Robert rushed to his side.

The church prayed. Media reported. And when we spoke to Dad on Sunday from his hospital bed, we felt relieved. Then Mom called, "The bleeding has returned. Robert's family needs him at home. The second surgery is tomorrow. Can you come be with me?"

I arrived the next day expecting Dad to be sitting up in bed, his usual verbose self, asking questions, eager to be out of there. Instead, he could not put two words together. My world suddenly reeled.

Back at the hotel that night, I found it hard to be strong for Mom. She was kneeling by the bed, praying for Dad, reading her Bible, and modeling for me tough faith for tough times. | SHEILA SCHULLER COLEMAN

WINDMILLS, WATSON RANCH, NEBRASKA, USA

Weakness to strength

"For Christ's sake, I delight in weaknesses, in insults, in hardships, in persecutions, in difficulties. For when I am weak, then I am strong."

2 CORINTHIANS 12:10

The Bible makes an astonishing promise—out of our weakness will come strength.

That's like saying where a bone was broken, it will knit, weld, and become stronger there than at any other point. Where the flesh was cut the skin will mend and form a scar that is tougher there than at any other point on the body.

Once when I was making a hospital call, a doctor pointed out a nurse who was walking down the hall and said to me, "She's the best nurse we have. She works hard and is so dedicated," Then, as an afterthought, he added, "That's because when she was a teenager she spent ten months in the hospital."

Do you want to live an emotionally healthy and spiritually happy life? Learn to handle the hurts that come your way. Turn your scars into stars!

ROBERT H. SCHULLER

COUNTRY ROAD, ST. ANNE, ILLINOIS, USA

Wired for connectivity

"May he turn our hearts to him."

1 KINGS 8:58

Almighty God, the Creator, is our Great Connector. He created us for one purpose—to worship him and to be in fellowship with him. He wired us spiritually to connect with him. Deep within our souls God placed a longing for him that can only be filled by him. Yet, too often we neglect to spend time with him. Or, when we do fall to our knees, he feels so far away.

There are disruptions that threaten to disconnect us from God. However, because he loves us so much, he has a connection correction that can and will repair the broken wires and bring us back into a positive, loving relationship with him.

Disconnected by guilt? Reconnect through grace!

Disconnected by fear? Reconnect through renewed faith!

Disconnected by a broken spirit? Reconnect through God's healing power!

| SHEILA SCHULLER COLEMAN

EBOR FALLS, NEW SOUTH WALES, AUSTRALIA

A healing touch

*"When she heard about Jesus,
she came up behind him in the crowd and touched his cloak."*

MARK 5:27

After World War II, the townspeople of one devastated city in England wanted to restore a large statue of Jesus that had stood for many generations in the city square as a symbol of Christ's help and guidance. Christ's hands were outstretched in an attitude of invitation. The words carved on the pedestal read: "Come to me." Master artists and sculptors worked for months to reassemble the figure. But they couldn't find enough fragments in the rubble to mend Christ's hands. Finally, someone suggested, "The sculptors can make new hands." The townspeople rejected the proposal. "Leave him without hands!" they said.

Christ commissions us to help others. But we cannot help them and they cannot help us if we are unwilling to risk sharing our problems. Take a risk. Open up your life to others. You'll be surprised how often love comes your way.

ROBERT A. SCHULLER

BATTLEFIELD SITE, PICKETT'S CHARGE, PENNSYLVANNIA, USA

Seeing yourself through God's eyes

*"...to love your neighbor as yourself
is more important than all burnt offerings and sacrifices."*

MARK 12:33

Leonardo da Vinci is quoted as saying, "I have offended God and mankind because my work didn't reach the quality it should have." When Dinah Shore was asked if she had any enemies, she replied, "I'm not crazy about me." And Abraham Lincoln told friends that he considered the address he gave at the Gettysburg battlefield "a flat failure."

These are only a few examples of people who were their own worst critics and I bring them up only to let you know that you are not alone if you struggle with self-doubt and feelings of inadequacy. Many of us have grown up learning to be self-critical and berating ourselves for our failures.

But that's not the way God sees you. He sees you as an individual created in his image. In God's eyes you have inestimable worth and value.

| ROBERT A. SCHULLER

MILLSTREAM FALLS, QUEENSLAND, AUSTRALIA

Worth the "weight"

"The Lord disciplines those he loves,
and he chastens everyone he accepts as his child."

HEBREWS 12:6

I like the story of the man who had a one-hundred-year-old grandfather clock with a huge weight at the bottom. He watched as the old clock pushed that weight back and forth, back and forth. One day he thought, "That's a terrible burden for such an old clock to bear." So he opened the glass case and lifted the huge weight off to relieve the old antique's burden.

"Why do you take my weight off?" the old clock asked.

The old man replied, "I know it's a burden to you."

Then the old clock exclaimed, "Oh, no! My weight is what keeps me going."

God lets us experience frustrations and burdens in life to help us learn patience, to cause us to depend more on him, and to teach us humility. It is often the "weights" that keep us going! | ROBERT H. SCHULLER

OCTOBER   339

CLOUDSCAPE, WESTERN AUSTRALIA, AUSTRALIA

Tune in to positive thoughts

"As the heavens are higher than the earth,
so are my ways higher than your ways and my thoughts than your thoughts."

ISAIAH 55:9

When my children were growing up, they often had sibling squabbles and frequently ended up pouting and sulking. When that happened, I would take my finger and brush it lightly across their forehead from one side to the other and tell them, "Your mind is like a radio. Right here is the dial." I would playfully switch their right ear and then the left one and say, "These are the tuning knobs. Why don't you tune the dial and pick up a happier channel?"

You and I have the power to choose the wave lengths we tune in to—wave lengths that generate harmony or disharmony within our minds.

Next time an uninvited and unwelcome negative thought comes into your mind, tune it out by tuning in to good thoughts! | ROBERT H. SCHULLER

SHIPWRECK CREEK, CROAJINGOLONG NATIONAL PARK, VICTORIA, AUSTRALIA

First seek agreement

"Let your word agree with theirs,
and speak favorably."

2 CHRONICLES 18:12

Early in ministry, I learned this fundamental communication principle: Begin a conversation with someone who seems to be an adversary by first focusing on what you agree on, whether it's a common interest like music or sports or a shared hope or hurt. This is the emotional soil where powerful communication is cultivated.

I was not taught this "art of communication" when I studied to be a preacher. And my first year as a preacher, I failed to win an audience. What I discovered, purely by accident, is that people don't want to be preached to; they want to be helped, honestly and sincerely.

That is the secret of effective communication. Start by being sensitive to the hurting and troubled heart. Share how positive faith has inspired, encouraged, and lifted your spirit. In the process, you'll win a friend for life.

ROBERT H. SCHULLER

THE PUMPKIN PATCH, VERMONT, USA

Lesson from a jack-o-lantern

"You are the light of the world."

MATTHEW 5:14

I've occasionally given a children's sermon around Halloween and have found that using a pumpkin to illustrate the parallel between how someone becomes a Christian and how a pumpkin becomes a jack-o-lantern works well with kids.

I tell them, "God picks you from the pumpkin patch, brings you in and washes all the dirt off. Then he cuts off the top and scoops out all the yucky stuff. He removes the seeds of doubt, hate, selfishness, and fear, and carves you a bright new smiling face. Then he puts his light inside you for the whole world to see."

Matthew said it like this: "You are the light of the world. A city on a hill cannot be hidden." Next time you see a jack-o-lantern, remember this: You are the light Christ wants to use to bring hope and joy to the world.

| ROBERT A. SCHULLER

FALL TRANQUILITY, MASSACHUSETTS, USA

There is no thrill like the thrill of making a new discovery.
God hides the greatest treasures in the places we least expect.

ROBERT H. SCHULLER

November

DELTA QUEEN, NATCHEZ, MISSISSIPPI, USA

From lariat to laughter

*"I will instruct you and teach you in the way you should go;
I will counsel you with my loving eye on you."*

PSALM 32:8

One of the great men of American history is the legendary Will Rogers. His big ambition in life was to be a circus cowboy. He was finally given an opportunity to perform in New York but his whole career hinged on one trick—a lariat trick. He was so excited to be in New York and performing for a large audience where he hoped his rope trick would make him famous. But he was so nervous that he lost control at a peak point and got tangled up in his own lariat. Everybody laughed.

Instead of panicking, Will quipped, "Gettin' tangled up in a rope ain't so bad—unless it's 'round your neck!'" Everybody laughed again and again.

In making this mistake, Will Rogers discovered a new talent in himself—the ability to make people laugh. And that discovery changed his destiny.

| ROBERT H. SCHULLER

OSSIPEE RIVER, MAINE, USA

Optimist or pessimist?

*"I remain confident of this:
I will see the goodness of the Lord in the land of the living."*

PSALM 27:13

A nine-year-old boy arrived home from school one day to find his father waiting for him holding the boy's report card; it was filled with poor grades. "What do you have to say about this?" his father asked.

"Well, Dad," the boy replied, "you can be proud of me. At least you know I haven't been cheating." Now there's an optimist!

Optimists expect the best possible outcomes and emphasize the most positive aspects of a situation. A pessimist tends to take the least hopeful view of a situation.

At the heart and soul of both positive thinking and possibility thinking is the same powerful optimism. Optimism is the all-empowering attitude that unfailingly delivers the energy to start something, stay with it, or bounce back and start over again after a disappointment.

Optimism or pessimism—it's your choice. | ROBERT H. SCHULLER

SUNSET, BREAKWATER LIGHTHOUSE, DELAWARE, USA

Insight of hindsight?

"For our light and momentary troubles
are achieving for us an eternal glory that far outweighs them all."

2 CORINTHIANS 4:17

On December 21, 1988, the Motown recording group The Four Tops finished a recording session later than they had planned and missed their flight from London's Heathrow Airport to New York's JFK Airport. Another English rocker, John Lyndon, and his wife Nora missed the same flight because Nora hadn't finished packing in time. Numerous others reported similar stories.

Before Pan American Flight 103 took off, these individuals tied their lives and futures to the idea of making that flight. But when Pan Am Flight 103 exploded over Lockerbie, Scotland, two hours later, they realized just the opposite: their lives and futures were theirs because they missed the flight.

Hindsight has a way of showing us that God's plans are bigger than ours. So don't be too hasty to draw conclusions when seemingly bad things happen. Only God knows how the story will end. | ROBERT A. SCHULLER

MISSISSIPPI RIVER, NAUVOO, ILLINOIS, USA

Wait with confidence

"Every word of God is flawless."

P R O V E R B S   3 0 : 5

As a young boy I would often have to wait for my mother to pick me up from school after my sports or music practices. And sometimes I'd wait...and wait...and wait. But I was confident of this one thing: My mother *would* come! I might be the last child to leave the school grounds, but I knew my mother would always be there.

In the same way, you can rest in the confidence of the promises of God because his promises are true. You can't rely on your feelings, because feelings come and go. You can't count on them. They will lead you astray, frequently fool you, and let you down.

God challenges you to live, trust, and believe the facts—the truths he's given you in his Word. You can trust them. You can count on them—every word!

| ROBERT A. SCHULLER

KIMBERLEY SAILING BOAT, WESTERN AUSTRALIA, AUSTRALIA

Lost and found

*"Those who live in accordance with the Spirit
have their minds set on what the Spirit desires."*

ROMANS 8:5

I wrote all morning, enjoying the ease of revising text on a word processor. Jason, my five-year-old, ran into the room, saw a red button and pushed it before I could stop him.

"No!"

Just like that my work disappeared.

Feeling sick within, I remembered my parents' admonition to look for a silver lining. Still, what good could come from losing all my work?

"Is it possible, Lord, you knew it would be better after a re-write when I was more painstaking than this morning? So be it."

I fed the boys lunch, put them down for naps, and tackled the chapter again. Words flowed faster with more richness than in the first draft.

The first reaction to trouble is still, "Yikes! No!" But believing God can use it for good never fails to encourage me to try again.

| SHEILA SCHULLER COLEMAN

POWER FOR LIFE DEVOTIONAL

SUNSET, LAKE BOOMANJIN, QUEENSLAND, AUSTRALIA

Trouble redeemed

[Jesus said,] 'I have told you these things, so that in me you may have peace.
In this world you will have trouble.
But take heart! I have overcome the world."

JOHN 16:33

So often trouble is only a part of a painful growing process—like a seed buried alive by a seemingly merciless fate under suffocating ground in a windowless place, until in supreme agony it ruptures into new life! This death, burial, pain is not trouble. It is the travail of new birth: "...unless a grain of wheat falls into the ground and dies, it remains alone; but if it dies, it produces much grain" (John 12:24).

When trouble breaks your heart and makes your knees buckle, and forces penitent tears from eyes sealed in prayer to Almighty God, then trouble may turn out to be the redeeming agony before new birth.

What kind of people do you think we would be if we never had any trouble? It is only when we lift heavy loads that we build hard muscles in body, mind, and soul. | ROBERT H. SCHULLER

HORSE RIDING, GLENWORTH VALLEY, NEW SOUTH WALES, AUSTRALIA

Prodigal daughter

"He went to his father…his father was filled with compassion,
threw his arms around him and kissed him."

LUKE 15:20

I was ten. My brother Bobby was six. He teased mercilessly. I'd finally had enough. I packed a pillowcase with necessities, stashing it beneath my bed. I left a note for Mom and Dad hidden in the napkin holder.

"Dear Mom and Dad, I'm running away. I'm not mad at you, but I can't take Bobby anymore. Don't worry, I'll be fine."

Later Dad came to my room. "Sheila, if a little girl ran away, where would she go?"

"Probably the park."

"Wouldn't she be scared and cold?"

"Not with a blanket and flashlight."

"Do you have a blanket and a flashlight?"

Whoops, they had found my note!

I felt relief. My rebellion was short-lived. Dad's protective arms and warm love sufficed to abort my straying. Likewise, why would I ever run from Jesus who loves and gave his life for me? | SHEILA SCHULLER COLEMAN

WATER LILIES, PROSPECT CREEK, QUEENSLAND, AUSTRALIA

Getting over your problems

"'There is hope for your future,' declares the Lord."

JEREMIAH 31:17

Spurgeon, the great Baptist minister, was talking to a farmer friend out in the country. He noticed a cow with its head over a stone wall looking out into the distance. Spurgeon asked the farmer, "Why is that cow looking over the wall?" And the farmer answered, "Because she can't see through it."

You're going to face problems in your lifetime—setbacks, rejections, disappointments, discouragements, and seeming unanswered prayers. God may seem distant. You may hit a stone wall or sink to a new low. So what do you do when that happens? Do what that cow did: Look over the problem. Look to Jesus. Keep your eyes fixed in the distance, your sight set on the goal. If you remember to do this, you can respond with great confidence to any problem that comes your way. | ROBERT H. SCHULLER

SUNSET, USA

Keep your eyes on Jesus

"Fix your eyes on Jesus, the pioneer and perfecter of your faith."

HEBREWS 12:2

When a jet approaches the deck of an aircraft carrier to land, the Landing Signal Officer (LSO) on deck radios the incoming pilot to "call the ball." The "ball" is a round, orange light reflected through a Fresnel lens on the left side of the deck. The steady, centered position of that ball of light is what guides the pilot to a safe landing on the deck. When the pilot tells the LSO, "I have the ball," it means he has sighted the ball of light and is using it to hone in on the flight deck. As the pilot approaches the deck, his eyes are fixed on one thing—the ball. It's what ensures him a safe landing.

Keep your eyes on Jesus. Look to him for guidance and help. And you'll land safely, even during the storms of life. | ROBERT A. SCHULLER

GLORIOUS RAINBOW, USA

Broken to beautiful

"Like clay in the hand of the potter, so are you in my hand."

JEREMIAH 18:6

The Royal Palace in Tehran, Iran, is unlike anything I've ever seen anywhere else in the world. As you walk through the grand entrance, you think the domed ceilings, side walls, and columns are covered with diamonds...until you discover that the rainbow of colors is actually small pieces of mirror, reflecting light.

When the palace was being built, the architects ordered mirrors from Paris to cover the entrance walls. But when the mirrors arrived, they found that the mirrors had all been broken during travel. They were ready to junk the pieces when one creative thinker suggested, "Maybe the walls will be more beautiful *because* the mirrors are broken." He took all the pieces and from them created a beautiful, abstract mosaic.

That's a picture of our lives. God takes all the broken pieces and creates something beautiful from them. | ROBERT H. SCHULLER

HOH RAINFOREST, OLYMPIC NATIONAL PARK, WASHINGTON, USA

Disabled through dis-ease?

"Which is easier: to say to this paralyzed man,
'Your sins are forgiven,' or to say, 'Get up, take your mat and walk'?"

MARK 2:9

Illness—either spiritual or physical—can be crippling and painful. Disease can mean living under the weight of discomfort, dis-ease, even outright pain. The Great Physician specializes in healing you when you are disabled by illness of all types.

Physical healing is a miracle, but spiritual healing is all the more remarkable and wondrous. Jesus healed many people of assorted ailments, but he said "What is more difficult—to tell a man to pick up his mat and walk—or tell a man his sins are forgiven?"

Jesus is powerful enough to heal you physically. But more importantly, he gave his life so that he could save your life for all eternity. If you are disabled through spiritual or physical dis-ease, go to the Great Physician and ask him to heal you—inside and out! | SHEILA SCHULLER COLEMAN

SHERBURNE LAKE, GLACIER NATIONAL PARK, MONTANA, USA

Unanswered prayers

"This is the confidence we have in approaching God:
that if we ask anything according to his will, he hears us."

1 JOHN 5:14

I was raised on possibility thinking. So, when fishing at the lake, I baited my hook and sat for hours in the sun believing if I thought *hard* enough I would catch a ten-pound bass. I kept repeating: "I'm going to catch a ten-pound bass. I'm going to catch a ten-pound bass"...ad infinitum.

I didn't pray *for* a fish—even if I had, I doubt God would have answered.

There were many times in my young life when I did pray similar things. I had a child's faith and prayed like I used positive thinking—as if using a magic wand.

Now, as an adult, I understand prayer is not a mantra. Rather it is intimate conversation with God, my Heavenly Father. Prayer aligns my will with God's. And his answers take on new dimension and life.

SHEILA SCHULLER COLEMAN

SPUD TRUCK, VICTOR, IDAHO, USA

Big potatoes

*"It is God who arms me with strength
and keeps my way secure."*

PSALM 18:32

Many farmers in Idaho raised potatoes. Once harvested, the potatoes were spread out and sorted according to size—big, medium, and small. Only after they'd been sorted and bagged were the potatoes loaded onto trucks. This was the method used by all Idaho farmers—except one. He never bothered to sort his potatoes and yet seemed to make the most money. Puzzled, a neighbor asked him, "What's your secret?"

"Simple," the farmer replied, "I just load my wagon with potatoes and take the roughest road to town. During the trip the small potatoes fall to the bottom, the medium ones settle in the middle, and the big potatoes rise to the top."

The same thing can be said of people. "Big potatoes" rise to the top on the rough roads of life. Tough times never last, but tough people do!

| ROBERT H. SCHULLER

FISHING BOAT, SCILLA, ITALY

"Use me, Lord"

"Dear children, let us not love with words or tongue
but with actions and in truth."

1 JOHN 3:18

How do you want to be remembered?

All of us think about that question from time to time. I would hope that after I die, people would say of me, "He was an encourager. He gave me hope and courage." I want to be a blessing.

Anybody can be a blessing. All you need are three things: A head, a heart, and hands. You need only be able to give a word, a look, a touch.

God needs you. He wants to use you. He wants you to put your faith into action. You can be a mind through which Christ thinks, a heart through which Christ loves, and hands through which Christ helps those in need.

Next time you say, "Use me, Lord," you'd better really be asking for that. God never turns down such a generous offer! | ROBERT H. SCHULLER

PELICANS, TERRIGAL, NEW SOUTH WALES, AUSTRALIA

Backwards doesn't count

"I press on to take hold of that for which Christ Jesus took hold of me."

PHILIPPIANS 3:12

My car broke down before leaving on a trip to Palm Desert. A good friend of mine who happened to be a Cadillac dealer insisted that I drive one of his brand new Cadillac Seville demonstrator cars. Was that fun! I started the engine, put the car in reverse, and couldn't believe what I saw. As I backed out of the driveway, suddenly the digital speedometer started flashing, registering the miles per hour I was going in reverse. For the first time in the history of the car industry in the United States there was a speedometer that registered backward speed.

In times of defeat, it's easy to think we're going backwards. Let's not count it! The secret of success is to look ahead. We must lay aside the negative weights and run with patience the race that's in front of us.

| ROBERT H. SCHULLER

FLAMINGOES, ABU DHABI, UAE

Congenial communication

"Her ways are pleasant ways, and all her paths are peace."

PROVERBS 3:17

Communication takes many forms. Whether it's in the classroom, in the kitchen, across the cell-phone airwaves, or through the mini-microphones of sophisticated satellites, it is important to ask: What is the message you are sending? Is the message understandable? What's the feeling you want to express? Can you accomplish this through an e-mail, or do you need to send a letter? Should you telephone, or make a date to talk face to face?

Para-verbal and nonverbal communication are important parts of your message. Eye to eye, face to face, an encouraging smile and open hand impact the message you hope to send. They set you up to close the communication, not with a period at the end of a sentence on a piece of paper, but with a warm handshake or even a sincere hug. | ROBERT H. SCHULLER

OLD FORD TRUCK, AMIDON, NORTH DAKOTA, USA

Simply follow

*"If anyone would come after me,
he must deny himself and take up his cross daily and follow me."*

LUKE 9:23

John the Baptist stood out in a crowd. It's safe to say he "marched to the beat of a different drummer." He didn't sound like anyone else—he was loud and dramatic. He didn't look like anyone else—he wore clothes made of camel hair. He didn't act like anyone else—he ate locusts and wild honey. He liked living close to nature where he could feel God's presence, hear God's voice, and read God's word.

We would do well to follow John's example. No, we don't have to withdraw into solitude. Or reject society's dress or diet. But we do need to free ourselves from the distractions that compete for our energy and attention. We must simplify our lives so that God can enter and take over.

What things are preventing you from following God? Pull free from them. Simply follow. | ROBERT A. SCHULLER

HAVASU FALLS, SUPAI, ARIZONA, USA

Loving others

"Glory, honor and peace for everyone who does good."

ROMANS 2:10

To love and be loved is risky business so to self-preserve, like an old desert turtle, we pull into our protective shell where it is safe. But the turtle hidden in his shell misses out—on touch, smiles, the joy that comes from loving and being loved. Chances are you know you need to risk it, but where do you start?

Begin by praying for one person to love. Ask God to open your eyes to someone who needs you as much as you need them. It might be a child in your neighborhood whose parents are overwhelmed with life. It might be a church member who is shut in and needs meals now and then. It might be a homeless person who needs a sandwich to carry them through the night.

Your love just might be the answer to someone's prayers today!

SHEILA SCHULLER COLEMAN

KING GEORGE FALLS, WESTERN AUSTRALIA, AUSTRALIA

Face of mercy

"May your mercy come quickly to meet us, for we are in desperate need."

PSALM 79:8

There are some human tragedies that defy the imagination: the death of a young child to cancer, the taking of innocent lives by terrorists, utter destruction caused by forces of nature. In catastrophes like these, it is nearly impossible for us to see God's goodness.

What can we say when there is no evidence of God's goodness in what has happened? Look for God's face. It's during times like this that God loves to show his face of mercy.

Nothing happens that isn't ultimately good for us, good for God, or good for someone else. If the tragedy is the result of sin or some terrible human blunder, then you can expect God's redeeming sympathy and the kiss of his tender mercy. And when God comes to comfort, you and I can endure anything. | ROBERT H. SCHULLER

OLD PANEY HOMESTEAD, GAWLER RANGES, SOUTH AUSTRALIA, AUSTRALIA

The house with gold windows

"I have learned the secret of being content in any and every situation."

PHILIPPIANS 4:12

A young boy from an impoverished family lived on a farm. He got up early every morning to help his father milk the cows. He'd look to the east and watch the sun rise, then turn to the west to see a beautiful home with gold windows. *Someday I'll travel to that home with gold windows*, he thought.

That day came. He packed a lunch and started hiking due west. After reaching the house he thought had gold windows, he knocked on the door and a woman answered. "Is this the house with the gold windows?" he asked.

"No," she replied, "but wait and I'll show it to you." As the sun was setting, the woman pointed due east and said, "There's the house with the gold windows!" To his surprise, he saw his own home.

God's blessings are right here, right now. | ROBERT A. SCHULLER

MALIBU PIER, CALIFORNIA, USA

Count your blessings

"I will make you into a great nation, and I will bless you;
I will make your name great, and you will be a blessing."

GENESIS 12:2

God *is* blessing you!" Being blessed is not something that happened in your past or that you have to wait to have happen in your future. Rather, you are already blessed and you are continuing to be blessed.

The challenge is in recognizing and counting our blessings no matter what we're facing. Yet when we stop to appreciate how God is blessing us, it is impossible to fear and worry. As the old praise song teaches, "Count your many blessings, name them one by one, and it will surprise you what the Lord has done."

Focus on your blessings. Thank God for what you have, and thank him for what you do not have! After all, some "blessings" are really burdens in disguise. God knows what's best for you, and he will only give you what will ultimately be a blessing! | POWER FOR LIFE BIBLE

JIM JIM FALLS, KAKADU, NORTHERN TERRITORY, AUSTRALIA

My gem, Jim

"A wife of noble character who can find?
She is worth far more than rubies."

PROVERBS 31:10

My biological clock ticking, I was immersed in ministry. I knew I wanted to get married and have children and wondered if God had a husband for me. So I decided to ask Dad to pray that God would send someone to love and treasure me.

Jim, an artist, joined the staff. He wasn't a Christian. We worked side by side as friends for two years. Then Jim accepted Jesus. My interest was in spiritually mature men, but Jim remained my friend. Then God took my breath away by revealing to me how Jim had matured into an amazing Christian man. We dated, fell in love, and planned our wedding day.

Before Dad escorted me to my new life as Jim's wife, I thanked God for my gem, Jim, my father, who prayed for me, and my Heavenly Father, who provided love for me. | SHEILA SCHULLER COLEMAN

EAST ORANGE, VERMONT, USA

Coincidence or blessing?

*"Surely you have granted him unending blessings
and made him glad with the joy of your presence."*

PSALM 21:6

Sometimes God's blessings are not immediately apparent.

An acquaintance told me about an incident that happened when he was on a long trip by car. He took a wrong turn, got lost, and pulled off the road to look at his map. After getting his bearings, the man prepared to pull back out on the road. At the last minute, for no real reason, he hesitated. As he did, a huge tractor-trailer barreled by. He hadn't seen the truck at all. Had he pulled out in front of it, he most certainly would have been killed instantly.

What made him stop? Some people would say it was a coincidence. But I know this man and the compassion he has for the poor and needy; he'd give you his last dollar if you needed it. I am convinced God was protecting his life. | ROBERT A. SCHULLER

HAY BALES, HARRODSBURG, KENTUCKY, USA

Thanks giving = thanks living

*"Honor the Lord with your wealth,
with the firstfruits of all your crops."*

PROVERBS 3:9

A pastor stood before his church congregation and said, "I've got some good news and some bad. The good news is the church has all the money it needs. The bad news is, it's still in your wallets."

It's amazing how a dollar never looks smaller than when it's in our paycheck, and never looks bigger than when we write our tithe check. But as we learn to relinquish control of our financial resources and step out in faith, our lives are changed and we experience unparalleled blessing.

Tithing is the most concrete way we have to honor God and express our love and thanksgiving to him. It demonstrates in a tangible way our faith *in* God, our love *for* God, and our desire to surrender *to* God.

Don't give because the church needs your money. Give to become a better person. | ROBERT A. SCHULLER

VICTORIAN HOME, CAPE MAY, NEW JERSEY, USA

The tyranny of discontent

"Godliness with contentment is great gain."

1 TIMOTHY 6:6

In our increasingly materialistic society, debt is at an all-time high. With the ever-increasing prices of homes and rent, coupled with the emphasis on excessive lifestyles and instant gratification inherent in today's society, the temptation to acquire "more" is wreaking havoc with our priorities. And the way to satisfy the hunger for instant gratification is typically through debt.

The eager anticipation of the coveted item, however, loses its magic once the bill arrives. As the interest accrues, the "blessing" morphs into a "curse"—a heavy burden that loses its value and siphons off some of the joy of everyday living.

You can be freed from the tyranny of discontent, and the debt that inevitably accompanies it. Adopt the attitude of gratitude. Count your blessings. And make a commitment to say "Thank you" to the one who made your blessings possible. | POWER FOR LIFE BIBLE

HORSESHOE FALLS, NIAGARA FALLS, CANADA

The law of reciprocity

"Give, and it will be given to you. A good measure, pressed down, shaken together and running over, will be poured into your lap. For with the measure you use, it will be measured to you."

LUKE 6:38

One of the laws of physics says that for every action, there is an equal and opposite reaction. This is true in the physical, as well as spiritual realm. When we reach out a helping hand to others, we set in motion a chain reaction that will eventually come back to bless us. It may not be evident right away but it will happen nonetheless.

These blessings may come in a number of ways. You may experience financial reward or be blessed with happiness and peace of mind. You may find others are drawn to you because of your giving attitude and you are never lacking for supportive, caring friends. However the blessings come, the moment you reach out, the wheels are set in motion for you to also share in the blessing.

It's true. You never lose what you give to others. | ROBERT A. SCHULLER

WAIMEA BEACH, OAHU, HAWAII

Acts of kindness

"But a Samaritan, as he traveled, came where the man was; and when he saw him, he took pity on him."

LUKE 10:33

Are you kind? Really kind?

Most of us have learned how to act kindly, even though we may not really feel kind inside. We may express our sympathy to those who are hurting, pat them on the back, and tell them that things will get better. But the kindness to which God calls us goes far beyond that. He calls us to a genuine kindness that often demands our time, our money, and our hearts.

Jesus told the Parable of the Good Samaritan to help us better understand what it means to be truly kind. Being kind isn't always easy. When we see someone in trouble, it's easier to hope someone else will stop and help than for us to help. God wants to produce in us the fruit of kindness. And he will if we let him. | ROBERT A. SCHULLER

CUMBERLAND FALLS, KENTUCKY, USA

The power of "thank you"

"It is good to praise the Lord and make music to your name,
O Most High."

PSALM 92:1

Think about the power of these two little words—*thank you!* One sincerely spoken *thank you* can change a person's demeanor from morose to merry almost as quickly as you can say the words.

Thanksgiving releases gratitude in our hearts and immunizes us from the pessimism and cynicism that is all around us. There is nothing more important to our mental, emotional, and spiritual well-being.

Here are ten things for which you can be thankful: *Answered prayer* on your behalf; *Habits*, good ones formed and bad ones broken; *Sins forgiven*; *Healing* from the secret hurts of your heart; *Life's storms*, those you've gone through and others that have passed you by; *Friends*, old and new; *Impossibilities* that became achievements; *Gifts* given and received; *Possibilities* yet to be discovered; and *Hope* that springs eternal.

Make thanksgiving an essential part of your life! | ROBERT H. SCHULLER

CABLE GRIST MILL, TENNESEE, USA

Daily doses

"Be joyful in hope, patient in affliction, faithful in prayer."

ROMANS 12:12

No matter what you are facing, a daily dose of faith can carry you through. How do you find faith when your world falls apart? Sometimes you have to say aloud, even if you don't feel it, "I believe! I believe! I believe!" Faith is more than a feeling; it is a choice, and when you can choose to make faith statements, in time the feelings will follow.

Additionally, prayer is an essential spiritual vitamin. But pray as Jesus taught in The Lord's Prayer. Start every prayer with praise: "Our Father in heaven, hallowed be your name" (Matthew 6:9). By beginning your prayers with praise, you refocus your attention on the power of God.

Positive prayer, positive faith, and a positive outlook can provide the spiritual nourishment that will keep you going no matter how difficult the path becomes. | POWER FOR LIFE BIBLE

TABLE MOUNTAIN, SOUTH AFRICA

Claim God's will and power

"God's grace was so powerfully at work in them all."

ACTS 4:33

In order to achieve God's purposes, all you need to do is allow him to work through your life. He kindles your passion. He keeps you motivated, enabling you to see his purposes through to completion. He gives you the will. And when the going gets tough, God provides the desire.

God supplies the power you need to make it to the finish line. He supplies every resource—the help, the strength needed to complete *his* task. When you seem to lack time, money, assistance, it is not you, but God, who provides.

Your part is to stay connected, to allow him to work through you. If you attempt to do it alone, count on running out of steam, out of will and power. Claim the promise of today's Bible verse now. | SHEILA SCHULLER COLEMAN

God gives endurance to match encounters.

ROBERT H. SCHULLER

December

DOCKER RIVER ROAD, KATA TJUTA, NORTHERN TERRITORY, AUSTRALIA

Ready for Christmas?

"Prepare the way for the Lord,
make straight in the desert a highway for our God."

ISAIAH 40:3

Have you noticed how the day after Thanksgiving it's like someone pulls a trigger and the countdown to Christmas begins?

You clean the house from top to bottom. Rearrange furniture to make room for the tree. Check the tree lights before stringing them from top to bottom. Bake all kinds of goodies for a myriad of holiday parties you're invited to attend. Create your gift list. Check it twice. Make multiple trips to the shopping mall. Shop 'til you drop. Wrap gifts. And set all kinds of holiday wheels in motion. So now are you ready for Christmas? Not quite!

The most important item on your Christmas "do to" list is to prepare yourself.

If you want Christmas to be a real "God thing," then take time to prepare your heart and life to receive the Infant King. | ROBERT A. SCHULLER

MONUMENT VALLEY, ARIZONA, USA

When God steps in

"They cried to the Lord in their trouble, and he saved them from their distress. He brought them out of darkness...and broke away their chains."

PSALM 107:13-14

There is nothing more difficult for strong people to admit and accept than the helplessness they feel when sudden dark times strike. Mature, responsible, intelligent people feel compelled to take personal responsibility and "manage things." It is very difficult for them to admit they can no longer handle things by themselves.

All of us feel out of control at one time or another. And feeling out of control is devastating because it's something we've rarely encountered! The last thing we want to do is admit our helplessness.

What drives this denial? The human ego has an infinite ability to rationalize. We don't want to admit we need help. But hurting hearts only find health and healing when they finally admit, with authentic humility, "I need help. I can't make it alone."

That's when God steps in. | ROBERT H. SCHULLER

CEDAR FALLS, HOCKING HILLS STATE PARK, OHIO, USA

A hope-filled youth

You have been my hope, Sovereign Lord, my confidence since my youth."

PSALM 71:5

My mother and father were God-fearing people. They read the Bible every day in our home, took us to church every Sunday, prayed for us, and we prayed with them at the dinner table and before going to bed at night. My parents played the piano and sang hymns with us. I remember sitting on the piano bench with my mother when I was a child learning to sing, "Jesus loves me this I know, for the Bible tells me so."

That's where my journey of faith began. It's why today I can testify to the verse in Scripture that says, "You have been my hope, Sovereign Lord, my confidence since my youth" (Psalm 71:5).

I had a happy childhood because it was filled with hope. And that hope gave birth to beautiful dreams. | ROBERT H. SCHULLER

FIRST LIGHT, TERRIGAL, NEW SOUTH WALES, AUSTRALIA

Too tired to pray

"When you ask, you must believe and not doubt."

JAMES 1:6

As the mother of four sons under seven, it was hard to find uninterrupted time for prayer and God's word in the morning. No matter how early I awakened or whether I was in the bedroom or the kitchen, the boys ran in laughing and playing. Attempting a quiet time was futile.

I tried reading and praying before bedtime, only to fall asleep, awaken later with my head on my arms resting on my Bible with no idea where my prayers left off.

Finally, I bought myself a nice journal to record special prayers. I began to date and write them down. Writing helped keep me awake then, and today it keeps me from being too distracted.

I have filled many journals chronicling God's faithfulness. I love to go back and read them and see how marvelously God answered prayer after prayer.

| SHEILA SCHULLER COLEMAN

EILEAN DONAN CASTLE, LOCH DUICH, SCOTLAND

Catch and release

"Why were you searching for me?
Didn't you know I had to be in my Father's house?"

LUKE 2:49

It was Jewish custom for 12-year-old boys to begin worshipping with the men in the temple during Passover. So, at the appointed time, Jesus accompanied his parents to Jerusalem. However, when the feast was over Jesus could not be found. Can you imagine how frantic they must have felt when it took three days to find him?

Finally, they discovered him sitting in the temple courts among the teachers dialoguing with them on a level that astonished all.

When God calls our children to faraway places or to put their lives on the line, we learn from this story that it is not our role to get in the way. God's power will sustain them. God's power will protect them. It is our role to teach them about God and then entrust them to God's mighty power and loving grace. | POWER FOR LIFE BIBLE

KING GEORGE FALLS, WESTERN AUSTRALIA, AUSTRALIA

A day of rest

"'There are six days when you may work,
but the seventh day is a day of sabbath rest, a day of sacred assembly."

LEVITICUS 23:3

Henry Ford hired an efficiency expert to find the non-productive people in his factory. "Tell me who they are," Ford said, "and I will fire them."

Later, the expert returned and reported that he'd found one such person. Every time I walk by his door he's sitting with his feet propped up on his desk. When I enter the room, he stands, shakes hands, we exchange words, and then he props his feet back up on his desk when I leave." When Henry Ford learned who the man was he said, "I can't fire him. I pay him to do that...nothing but think!"

Six days is enough to jar, jade, smear, and stain anyone's moral ideals. We need one day in seven to have our ideals, hopes and dreams restored! Sunday was created for that. Let it be your day of *rest*. | ROBERT H. SCHULLER

LONE WINDMILL, SCOTTS BLUFF, NEBRASKA, USA

Epiphany

"If you declare with your mouth, 'Jesus is Lord,' and believe in your heart that God raised him from the dead, you will be saved."

ROMANS 10:9

When Albert Einstein conceived the mathematical equation $E=MC^2$ he had an epiphany. What is an epiphany? It's one of those moments in life when something profound is revealed to you. It's an "ah-ha" moment—the light goes on, you see and understand something you haven't seen or understood before, and the revelation you have in an instant forever changes your life.

We have epiphanies all the time. Our epiphanies might not have as great an impact as Einstein's theory of relativity, but they're epiphanies just the same.

Jesus came to earth to reveal who God the Father is—"the Word was made flesh and dwelt among us" (John 1:14). The most important epiphany you will ever have is seeing the message in the Messenger and saying without reservation, "Here is the Christ, the Son of the Living God."

| ROBERT A. SCHULLER

SUNRISE, EDDYSTONE POINT, TASMANIA, AUSTRALIA

Tap into word power

*"Grow in the grace and knowledge
of our Lord and Savior, Jesus Christ."*

2 PETER 3:18

In the beginning was the Word," begins John's gospel. The *Word* is God, Jesus, and the Holy Spirit. How powerful is Jesus, the Word! How powerful is God's word, the Bible, giving voice to God's thoughts. God's message is: God loves you and has a wonderful plan for your life!

The Word is life. The life is the light, which shines in the darkness. The darkness cannot overcome it. Tap into the power of God's word. Read it, pray it in Jesus' name.

Share the power of the Word with others. We were not created for God's transforming power to end with us. We are to be conduits of God's powerful message to those lost in darkness. The more we read God's word, the more we pray, the more we share the Word with others, the more powerful our lives will be. | SHEILA SCHULLER COLEMAN

GIRL AND COW, TASMANIA, AUSTRALIA

No refuge in money

"You cannot serve both God and money."

MATTHEW 6:24

Where do you turn for refuge during difficult financial times? Many people turn to money. But there's no security in money; it can be wiped out overnight.

Every so often, the stock market behaves like a runaway roller coaster heading downhill. Millions of dollars are lost. So-called experts term this a "hiccup" and say that the market is readjusting itself. But one severe hiccup can wipe out the life savings of hundreds of small investors.

Money is a "false god." It is not a savior. There is nothing wrong with having money unless you come to think of it as the most important thing in life or as the means of giving you the security you seek. Money will always let you down.

Faced with a financial downturn? Take refuge in God. Trust him.

| ROBERT A. SCHULLER

BIKE RIDING, TASMANIA, AUSTRALIA

The gift of time

"My times are in your hands."

PSALM 31:15

I t was a day much like any other. We sent Anthony off to school, expecting to see him again around two o'clock that afternoon. I went about my business, only to have my plans change fifteen minutes later when a neighbor pulled into our driveway with Anthony in the front seat. He was crying and holding his ear. His bicycle was in the trunk. Anthony had fallen off his bike and hit his ear hard enough to cause a hematoma. We headed for the doctor's office...and from there went to a surgeon's office where they operated on Anthony's ear to remove the hematoma.

So often we think that we control our own time—the days, the hours, the minutes. When, in fact, time is on loan to us from God. It's a gift. Thank him for it. And make good use of it. | ROBERT A. SCHULLER

HAMERSLEY NATIONAL PARK, WESTERN AUSTRALIA, AUSTRALIA

A cut above

"God will save his people on that day...
They will sparkle in his land like jewels in a crown."

ZECHARIAH 9:16

There was a king who owned a large, perfectly cut diamond. He was so proud of it that he made it his country's national symbol. One day he discovered that the stone's beauty was marred by a long, hair-like scratch.

The king sent word throughout the kingdom, "Whoever can restore the stone to its former beauty will be rewarded."

The king was ready to give up hope when a poor lapidary called on him.

"Sir, this scratch that has diminished the diamond's worth will become its most beautiful asset," the lapidary promised.

Weeks passed. Then one day the lapidary returned. When he opened the velvet box, the king gasped in amazement. There was the stone, more exquisite than ever, with a beautiful rose carved on it, the stem disguising its fatal flaw.

God can take your "scratches" and transform them into exquisite assets.

| ROBERT A. SCHULLER

SUNRISE, FRESHWATER BEACH, NEW SOUTH WALES, AUSTRALIA

Miracle-working power

"Because of the Lord's great love we are not consumed, for his compassions never fail. They are new every morning; great is your faithfulness."

LAMENTATIONS 3:22-23

Miracles happen every day. God rescues, saves, redeems, and heals his children. In fact, many miracles go unnoticed. That's because God rarely works instantaneous miracles. He's not a genie we summon to perform and entertain. He is a sovereign God who has built into his creation healing properties. He has already set in motion forces to provide for all our needs.

As such, it is not uncommon for his miracles to take time. Frequently, his miracle-working power takes years as he heals us cell by cell. We walk by his miracle-working power daily, failing to recognize the miracles for what they are: flowers blooming, sunshine warming our earth, loved ones being reconciled after bitter disputes, an encouraging phone call from a family member.

Open your eyes today to see and recognize the miracle-working power of God in your life! | SHEILA SCHULLER COLEMAN

ST. JOSEPH'S CHURCH, ALBANY, WESTERN AUSTRALIA, AUSTRALIA

The original promise keeper

"For to us a child is born…and he will be called Wonderful Counselor,
Mighty God, Everlasting Father, Prince of Peace."

ISAIAH 9:6

Between 739 and 680 B.C., the prophet Isaiah foretold that the Messiah would be born. Among the details given were these:

The Messiah would be God's son.

He would be born of a virgin in Bethlehem.

He would save the Israelites from oppressors.

He would be of the house of David.

He would be despised and rejected by men, a man of sorrows, and familiar with suffering.

All the Israelites, who knew the prophecies of Isaiah, longed for and prayed for the Messiah to come quickly because their lives were hard.

And all these prophesies came true, each given not only to reassure us that Jesus was indeed the long-awaited Messiah, but also to assure us that our God is an upright, trustworthy God who always keeps his promises.

| POWER FOR LIFE BIBLE

SWIFT CURRENT LAKE, GLACIER NATIONAL PARK, MONTANA, USA

Silent, strong, prayerful presence

"[God] does not take his eyes off the righteous;
he enthrones them with kings and exalts them forever."

JOB 36:7

Imagine the shock and betrayal Joseph must have felt when he found out his fiancée, Mary, was pregnant. Joseph could have denounced her shamefully. But because he was a "righteous man" (Matthew 1:19), he resolved to not only do the right thing, but to do it in a loving way.

It's easy to take people like Joseph for granted. He was a virtuous man who loved his wife and children, worked hard, and made an honest living to support his family and make the world a better place.

The power of Joseph's life was that "he did what the angel of the Lord had commanded him" (Matthew 1:24). He was willing to do God's will no matter what it cost him.

All it takes is a silent, strong presence to make the difference in someone's life. | POWER FOR LIFE BIBLE

A PAINTING OF THE WISE MEN, SAINT THEODOSIOS MONASTERY, HOLY LAND

Open-heart power

"When they saw the star, they were overjoyed. On coming to the house, they saw the child…and they bowed down and worshiped him."

MATTHEW 2:10-11

Bethlehem was a town in Judea. Herod, the King of Judea, was troubled when asked by wise men from the East, "Where is he who has been born the King of the Jews? We saw his star when it rose and have come to worship him."

Imagine how unsettling that question was for Herod. He had no intention of giving up his power to any other king. Herod was willing to kill for power.

But God's plan was that the most powerful king to ever reign would be a merciful and loving king who would bring life versus death—a King of Kings who was his Son, Jesus Christ. The good news is that Jesus was born, he lived died, and rose again, and he reigns today in every heart that welcomes him in

| POWER FOR LIFE BIBLE

FRESCO IN THE SHEPHERDS' FIELD CHURCH, NEAR BETHLEHEM, HOLY LAND

The glory of Christmas

"The Word became flesh and made his dwelling among us."

JOHN 1:14

In the opening scene of the musical *Camelot*, King Arthur is standing in a field dressed as a peasant. No one knows he is the king.

That is what God did for us. The King of Kings set aside his heavenly robes and divine prerogatives and came to earth to live as one of us. He ate with us, drank with us, felt with us. He spoke his mind, declared his will, and revealed his heart.

Why did he do this? Because he wanted us to know what God is really like. For God and man to have an eternal relationship, a sacrifice for sin had to be made. God's love compelled Jesus to be that sacrifice.

God loved the world so much that he sent his only Son to earth—not to condemn it, but to save it. That's the glory of Christmas!

ROBERT A. SCHULLER

SUNRISE OVER BETHLEHEM, HOLY LAND

God's glorious portrait

"God has chosen to make known...the glorious riches of this mystery,
which is Christ in you, the hope of glory."

COLOSSIANS 1:27

For years, mankind searched for God. Often they lost him. Frequently they misunderstood him—they thought he was to be feared, ignored and rejected. They created impressions of what they thought God was which led them so far astray, God made the ultimate sacrifice—he came to earth as a baby. He was born to a common woman on a cold night in a dirty cave that was used as an animal stall.

This tiny baby was God in human form. His name was Jesus. As he grew he began to fulfill his mission...to show the world what God is really like. In Jesus, we see a God who is loving, tender, caring, and forgiving. We see a God who embraced the people society rejected. He restored their dignity Jesus painted a glorious portrait of God so we could do the same.

| ROBERT H. SCHULLER

SUNRISE OVER THE SEA OF GALILEE, MOUNT OF BEATITUDES, ISRAEL

It's all good

"Glory to God in the highest heaven,
and on earth peace to those on whom his favor rests."

LUKE 2:14

Angels serve many roles, but in the scriptures they are most frequently seen as messengers, usually delivering good news. When Jesus was born, the angels delivered the news that this baby was special—first to Mary, then to Joseph, and finally to the populace through shepherds.

Anyone can be an angel—not literally, but figuratively—if you are a messenger of God. It doesn't take angel wings to share the good news that Jesus is the Messiah, God's Son, born that we might have life and have it more abundantly.

Good news is always appreciated. People avoid those who only share bad news, but are drawn to people who bear good news. What good news will you share today? Make a commitment to be an angel and share the good news of God's love and grace today and every day! | POWER FOR LIFE BIBLE

CHIMNEY ROCK, NEBRASKA, USA

Parked by the flag pole

"If you remain in me and my words remain in you,
ask whatever you wish, and it will be done for you."

JOHN 15:7

After delivering a speech at a big convention hall, the man who was going to take me to the hotel walked with me to the parking lot. He said his car was parked by the buses. But no buses were to be found. After walking the two-acre parking lot, we finally found the car. The driver breathed a sigh of relief and said, "Next time I'm going to park by the flag pole."

Until you are irrevocably committed to Jesus Christ, you are parked by the buses. An alluring voice here, a charming voice there calls out, "Come on, try it." And you'll follow because you aren't anchored to anything.

Make Jesus Christ the flag pole of your life. He lived and died and rose again, so that you always know the place you can return to. Give your life to him. | ROBERT H. SCHULLER

PIONEER FARM, TWIN FALLS STATE PARK, WEST VIRGINIA, USA

Home for Christmas

"Come to me, all you who are weary and burdened,
and I will give you rest."

MATTHEW 11:28

Someone once said that *home is where you go and they have to take you in.* I've also heard the saying, *"Home is where you go when you're lonely, feeling sick, or are hurting."*

To "come home," you have to have been away. For some it means coming home from war. For others it may mean coming home from work. Some are coming home from wandering—they've been away from God like the Prodigal Son.

Home is the only place to go when nobody else understands. It's where you go to cry your heart out, knowing you won't feel embarrassed or ashamed. Home is where you can go and not be lonely. God invites you this Christmas to come home to him.

Wherever you are today, I invite you to come home. The Father is waiting with arms wide-stretched to welcome you. | ROBERT H. SCHULLER

HORSEPASTURE RIVER, NANTAHALA NATIONAL FOREST, NORTH CAROLINA, USA

Redemptive, unconditional love

"How priceless is your unfailing love, O God!"

PSALM 36:7

Imagine a husband-to-be standing at the altar, exchanging wedding vows with a woman he loves with all his heart, even knowing she will commit adultery over and over. Imagine knowing that other men will father some of the children she will bear and having to explain to them why their mother never comes home anymore. Then—imagine him taking her back, caring for her, and loving her—after all that!

Such was the life of the prophet Hosea.

Our hearts tend to be faithless and we often withdraw and hold back our love from God. But his love toward us never changes. God doesn't offer us a one-time-only chance at his love. He continues to love us—regardless!

God loves us unconditionally. Let his love sink deep into your spirit. His love, mercy, and grace are there for *you*! | POWER FOR LIFE BIBLE

AVOCA BEACH, NEW SOUTH WALES, AUSTRALIA

The cross

"For the message of the cross is foolishness to those who are perishing, but to us who are being saved it is the power of God."

I CORINTHIANS 1:18

"When I survey the wondrous cross!"

"Amazing grace how sweet the sound!"

"I know that my Redeemer lives!"

There is no more powerful message than that of the cross. At the foot of the cross, on your face in gratitude, you have assurance the Holy Spirit within gives you to live abundantly. Knowing you are loved deeply and widely, you find a desire to use that power by stepping out in faith. It is in knowing forgiveness that you find freedom to dream of becoming the person God designed you to be.

The cross is the source of true power—the power that comes from knowing you are loved and forgiven by your merciful, loving Creator. Say yes today to being used as a conduit of the power of Christ. There is no better way to live! | SHEILA SCHULLER COLEMAN

SANDSTONE ARCH, VALLEY OF FIRE STATE PARK, NEVADA, USA

Disconnected by grief?

*"Jesus cried out...'My God, my God,
why have you forsaken me?'"*

MATTHEW 27:46

Loss of a loved one can bring inconsolable grief, disconnecting you from God if you blame him for the loss. Nobody experienced more profound grief than God. He sent his Son to die on the cross knowing they would be separated for the only time throughout eternity when Christ took your sins upon himself.

Even though God could have prevented it by sending an army of angels to rescue Jesus from crucifixion, he allowed Christ to suffer spiritual and physical agony so that you could reconnect with God. If anyone knows grief—it's God. But his love for you surpassed even the grief of allowing his Son to die on the cross.

Your grief can be erased by the joy of knowing God loved you enough to sacrifice his Son's life for you. There is no greater love—no greater joy!

| SHEILA SCHULLER COLEMAN

PEMAQUID POINT, MAINE, USA

Make your life count

"In Joppa there was a disciple named Tabitha...
she was always doing good and helping the poor."

ACTS 9:36

Annie J. Flint penned the wonderful words to this well-known poem.

Christ has no hands but our hands to do his work today;
He has no feet but our feet to lead men on their way;
He has no tongue but our tongues to tell men how he died;
He has no help but our help to bring them to his side.

Jesus needs you and me to tell the world about him! He doesn't ask us to do this all alone; he promises that he will be there, helping us along the way. It is not our responsibility to change hearts, but it is our responsibility to share the Good News. God will take it from there.

Make your life count—be the hands, the voice, the feet of Jesus to somebody today. | POWER FOR LIFE BIBLE

SALT FLAT, GUADALUPE MOUNTAINS, TEXAS, USA

Live in God's favor

"Now is the time of God's favor, now is the day of salvation."

2 CORINTHIANS 6:2

My son Robby is a tremendous young man. He has the spirit of Jesus and people who meet him appreciate him for that. He says he has God's favor—and that's the way he lives.

Robby often tells me about all the wonderful things that have happened to him because he has God's favor. Who of us doesn't want God's favor?

When the angels announced the Good News of Jesus' birth, they sang, "Glory to God in the highest, and on earth peace to men on whom his *favor* rests" (Luke 2:14). The key to peace is achieved through understanding and having God's favor.

Right now stop and say these words out loud: "I have God's favor." God's favor rests on everyone who is a member of God's family. Live as God's favored child today. | ROBERT A. SCHULLER

RIO GRANDE, BIG BEN NATIONAL PARK, TEXAS, USA

The greatest gift

"The Lord appeared...saying: 'I have loved you with an everlasting love;
I have drawn you with unfailing kindness.'"

JEREMIAH 31:3

In December 1984, the day after what had been the gloomiest Christmas Day of my life, I went for a walk on the beach in spite of overcast skies and mist. There was only one other person on the beach that day, a woman named Donna. We began talking as we walked along. I told her I was married with two children. She asked me what a family man was doing on the beach alone on the day after Christmas. I explained that I was separated and would soon be divorced. Her situation was identical to mine.

We met together several times after that to talk, swapped books, and found comfort in the similarity of our circumstances. I found myself drawn to this lovely woman. In due course, Donna became my wife and has, over the past twenty plus years, become God's greatest gift of love to me.

| ROBERT A. SCHULLER

ST. MICHAEL'S MOUNT, CORNWALL, UK

Who me?

"Pride brings a person low,
but the lowly in spirit gain honor."

PROVERBS 29:23

What was God thinking–calling little ol' me to such a noble task? There's no way I'm up to this! I am incapable–unworthy–unskilled–inept. I can think of many others who would be far more suited for this calling.

Ah, but God never makes mistakes. He frequently calls the least likely for a task. That way, when all is said and done, you can't take credit for it. You can't get a big head because you know–better than anyone–how much you had to rely on God.

Also, you look back and see how much you have grown and learned about yourself, about your Creator, about your faith, because you were not capable of doing this alone.

Who me? Who else? *You* have been specifically called and chosen by the God of the Universe. | SHEILA SCHULLER COLEMAN

PADRE BAY, LAKE POWELL, UTAH, USA

Stepping on the scale

*"Let us hold unswervingly to the hope we profess,
for he who promised is faithful."*

HEBREWS 10:23

Faith confronts reality; it doesn't run away from it.

I remember a time when I had put on some extra pounds. I prayed for guidance. The message was loud and clear: "Step on the scale every day." So I started doing that...and writing down my weight. And I succeeded in taking off those extra pounds!

Are you facing a challenge similar to this? Begin by saying, "I will begin to affirm myself by being honest. I'm going to stop kidding myself because I don't want to cheat myself. And I'm cheating myself if I'm not being honest."

Today "step on the scale." Begin to turn your life around. Face up to your reality. Approach your situation without fear, knowing that with God all things are possible.

The little things you do today will add up to a lifetime of joy!

| ROBERT H. SCHULLER

WHITSUNDAY ISLANDS, QUEENSLAND, AUSTRALIA

Keep your goal in sight

"Run in such a way as to get the prize."

1 CORINTHIANS 9:24

Florence Chadwick wanted to be the first woman to swim from Catalina Island to the California coast. She dreamed about it, planned for it, and prepared for it. Finally the day came. She got into the water and began swimming. The sea was like an ice bath and the fog so dense she could hardly see her support boats. After sixteen hours of agonized swimming, she was utterly spent. She begged a spotter boat to lift her out of the water. Later she discovered she had come within half-a-mile of the fogged-in shoreline.

As Florence told a reporter, "I could have made it had I been able to see land. I will swim it again." Two months later, Florence Chadwick tried again.. this time she made it!

So can you. Set your dreams. Establish your goals. Then go for it!

| ROBERT H. SCHULLER

DERBY RACES, WESTERN AUSTRALIA, AUSTRALIA

The finish line

"My grace is sufficient for you, for my power is made perfect in weakness."

2 CORINTHIANS 12:9

So close! The finish line is within reach! Onlookers are cheering! Yet, this can be the most trying time of all—the time when energy betrays you, when you let down ever so slightly, perhaps even lying down, never to cross the finish line. Maybe you are just out of gas. It took so much for you to launch, more to overcome the obstacles, and now you feel as though you have nothing left.

Now, more than ever, you need to shout out to your Creator for extra steam. You cannot do this alone. Your energy is limited. Your batteries cannot carry you the distance. You must call upon the ultimate power source when the finish line is within reach. "Keep me going, Lord! Help me to finish strong!"

Can you feel the heavenly throng cheering you on to finish strong?

SHEILA SCHULLER COLEMAN

TREE FERN, TARA BULGA NATIONAL PARK, VICTORIA, AUSTRALIA

Time to shout hallelujah!

"And they cried out in a loud voice:
'Salvation belongs to our God, who sits on the throne, and to the Lamb.'"

REVELATION 7:10

In the last book of the Bible—the Revelation of John—the apostle John, while exiled on the island of Patmos, wrote about a vision he had of heaven. In this vision, John described multitudes of people from every nation standing before a throne. They were wearing white robes, holding palm branches, and shouting praises to the Lamb (Revelation 7:9-10).

We may not understand this, but it's going to be exciting to one day stand directly in God's presence. Being directly in God's presence is going to be the highest high anyone could ever experience.

In this life, we don't often get a full sense of God's presence. Yet every now and then God gives us a small taste of what it's like to be near him. Imagine experiencing that forever. You will, if you've invited Christ to be your Savior and Lord. | ROBERT A. SCHULLER